Turning Points: Key Moments in Human History

Arjun Gupta

Copyright © [2023] by Arjun Gupta

TITLE: Turning Points: Key Moments in Human History

AUTHOR: Arjun Gupta

All rights reserved.

No part of this publication may be reproduced, stored in a retrieval system, or transmitted, in any form or by any means, electronic, mechanical, photocopying, recording, or otherwise, without the prior written permission of the publisher.

ISBN: 978-93-5868-833-7

Table Of Content

Chapter 1: The Agricultural Revolution　　　　　　　　　05
- Introduction to the significance of the Agricultural Revolution
- Exploration of the shift from hunter-gatherer societies to settled agricultural communities
- Examination of key developments such as the domestication of plants and animals
- Impact on social structures, technology, and human civilization

Chapter 2: The Renaissance and the Age of Discovery　　35
- Overview of the Renaissance as a cultural and intellectual revival
- Exploration of the Age of Discovery and major expeditions
- Discussion of the impact of new knowledge and global exploration on society
- Examination of key figures like Leonardo da Vinci, Christopher Columbus, and others

Chapter 3: The Industrial Revolution　　　　　　　　　60
- Introduction to the technological advancements and societal changes during the Industrial Revolution
- Exploration of key inventions and their impact on manufacturing and transportation
- Analysis of the social and economic consequences, including urbanization and the rise of capitalism
- Examination of the role of industrialization in shaping the modern world

Chapter 4: World Wars I and II　　　　　　　　　　　　90

- Overview of the causes and consequences of World War I
- Examination of the interwar period and the lead-up to World War II
- In-depth analysis of key events, battles, and strategies during both wars
- Discussion of the profound social, political, and economic changes resulting from the wars

Chapter 5: The Digital Revolution and the Information Age   117
- Introduction to the rise of digital technology and its impact on communication and information sharing
- Exploration of key milestones in the development of computers, the internet, and other technological innovations
- Analysis of the societal changes brought about by the Information Age
- Discussion of the challenges and opportunities presented by the digital revolution

Conclusion: 142
- Summarization of the key turning points in human history explored in the book
- Reflection on the interconnectedness of these moments and their lasting impact on the world
- Consideration of potential future turning points and their implications for humanity

Chapter 1: The Agricultural Revolution

○ Introduction to the significance of the Agricultural Revolution

Introduction
Nomadic hunter-gatherer tribes gave way to agricultural settlements marked by the Agricultural Revolution, a watershed event in human history. This revolutionary upheaval, which began around 10,000 BCE, reshaped economies, cultures, and the entire fabric of human existence. More than just a change in farming methods, the Agricultural Revolution had far-reaching effects that continue to ripple through history and shape our modern world.

The First Farms and Their Impact on the World
Understanding the historical context of the Agricultural Revolution is essential before diving into its significance. The cradle of agriculture is frequently connected to the Fertile Crescent, an area in the Middle East containing parts of present-day Iraq, Syria, Lebanon, Israel, and Jordan. This is where early humans first began farming cereal grains and domesticating animals like sheep and goats. It was a huge step forward from the precarious hunter-gatherer existence to be able to take charge of one's own food supply through careful management of the environment.

As time went on, other areas began to practice agriculture after its initial success in the Fertile Crescent. It was in China that rice was first cultivated, in Mesoamerica it was maize, and in the Andes it was potatoes. This worldwide spread of agriculture paved the way for the development of many different cultures, each of which improved upon previous methods by tailoring them to its specific climate and topography.

The Transition from Nomadism to Urbanization

The transition from nomadic, hunter-gatherer lives to settled farming societies was one of the most obvious and transformational results of the farming Revolution. Growing food allowed people to settle down for the long haul, which paved the way for the development of towns and then cities. The ability to settle down and create permanent structures meant that the social order could benefit greatly from this shift from nomadic existence.

The sedentary way of life facilitated the growth of expertise in particular fields. Hunting and gathering were essential life skills in a nomadic culture. However, with the security that agriculture brought, people were able to devote themselves to learning specialized skills, which spawned new professions and laid the groundwork for sophisticated social structures.

The Urbanization of a Growing Population

The Agricultural Revolution had a crucial part in generating enormous population expansion. Communities might support higher populations if they had access to a more consistent and plentiful food supply. This spike in population ultimately pushed the development of complex civilizations.

Larger and more intricate cities sprang up as people increased. Towns sprang from villages, and those grew into cities. The concentration of humans in urban regions constituted a watershed moment in human history, as it allowed for the freer flow of information, goods, and even technologies. The synergy between agriculture and urbanization became a stimulus for the development of great civilizations.

Changes in the Surplus and Trade in the Economic System
Agriculture not only ensured survival, but also resulted in an abundance of edible goods. This excess was a game-changer, since it allowed society to collect reserves that could be used during times of scarcity or sold with adjacent tribes. Communities began exchanging agricultural surplus for other commodities and services as surplus became commonplace. Because of this monetary interconnectedness, complex trading networks were established between previously unconnected areas.

The establishment of trade channels allowed for the dissemination of ideas, as well as the transfer of goods. Economies became more varied as societies developed specialized approaches to farming and manufacturing. The surplus agricultural production allowed for economic diversification that aided the growth of civilizations and facilitated globalization.

Developments in Technology
The Agricultural Revolution was a driving force in the development of both the economy and new technologies.

Plows, irrigation systems, and better seed selection all arose as a result of the demand for more effective agricultural techniques and tools. As a result of these innovations, agricultural output rose, allowing cultures to accommodate greater populations.

More than that, the wealth created opportunities for new schools and learning hubs to open. Agricultural practices, animal husbandry, and irrigation methods were meticulously documented and transmitted from one family to the next. The advancement of human civilization may be traced in large part to the basis of scientific and technological progress that was laid by the collection of agricultural knowledge.

Changes in Society and Culture
The Agricultural Revolution was not just significant economically and technologically, but also culturally and socially. The sedentary lifestyle supported the development of sophisticated social structures, with leaders forming to manage and oversee the more intricate affairs of burgeoning communities. Because of the food excess, non-farming experts could be supported, which eventually led to the development of formalized social stratification systems.

Many agrarian communities also experienced a shift in their religious beliefs, as gods came to represent the sun and rain, two factors essential to agricultural success. The cultural identity of these communities was shaped by the rituals and ceremonies that were connected with the cyclical rhythm of agricultural seasons. Because solid and well-defined areas were needed for agricultural purposes, property rights and territorial limits also rose to prominence.

Effects on the Environment

The Agricultural Revolution resulted in remarkable improvements, but it also had serious consequences for the natural world. Deforestation, caused by humans making room for farmland, has altered ecosystems and reduced biodiversity. Monoculture farming practices accelerated soil degradation and erosion. Changing ecosystems and even overgrazing in some areas are direct results of the domestication of animals for agricultural purposes.

The agrarian revolution's effects on the environment show how intricately human cultures are intertwined with the natural world. Humanity's power to change and manipulate the environment to satisfy its needs has come with the responsibility of minimizing the disruption of natural processes.

Conclusion

The importance of the Agricultural Revolution, in conclusion, is huge. This pivotal era in human history paved the way for the development of civilizations, which in turn shaped the world in which we now find ourselves. From the move from nomadism to settlement, population increase, and urbanization, to economic transformations, scientific improvements, and cultural and social alterations, the repercussions of the Agricultural Revolution are embedded in the very fabric of our civilizations.

To fully appreciate the magnitude of agriculture's impact, we must acknowledge the positive and negative outcomes it produced. While the Agricultural Revolution catapulted humanity into a new era of creativity and connection, it also caused environmental effects that have had lasting effects on our interaction with the natural world. Recognizing the Agricultural Revolution's multidimensional importance helps us comprehend the richness of our common history and provides a platform for tackling the modern difficulties that arise from our interactions with the environment and one another.

- **Exploration of the shift from hunter-gatherer societies to settled agricultural communities**

  The shift in human history from nomadic hunter-gatherer tribes to sedentary agricultural cultures is a watershed moment. Over the course of several centuries, the basic basis of human existence was altered as a result of what has been known as the Agricultural Revolution. Leaving behind nomadic, subsistence-based living for settled agricultural societies required more than just a shift in economic patterns; it also represented a radical reorientation of human society as a whole. In this investigation, we delve into the complexities of this shift by looking at what sparked it, what obstacles it presented, and what far-reaching effects it has on modern communities.

  The Nomadic Hunter-Gatherer Way of Life
  Hunting, fishing, and gathering were vital to human subsistence before to the development of agriculture. This nomadic culture consisted of tiny bands of people that traveled from place to place in quest of resources, typically following the movements of animals and the harvesting of plants. This manner of existence, albeit deeply connected with the natural environment, was defined by its unpredictability and the constant need for mobility.

  Adaptability to a wide range of climates, from dry deserts to humid rain forests, was a hallmark of hunter-gatherer cultures. They learned to make extensive use of the indigenous flora and wildlife, including for sustenance, clothing, and shelter. However, because of their reliance on wild resources, these communities were vulnerable to the whims of Mother Nature. Famine and forced migration are possible outcomes of unsuccessful hunting or a shortage of food sources.

Environmental and demographic pressures are the catalysts for change.
The eventual abandonment of hunter-gathering was caused by a number of interrelated circumstances. Environmental factors, such as climate change and the loss of easily accessible resources, had a key influence. Diminishing returns in terms of accessible food sources occurred when populations developed and ranged over broader territory, putting greater stress on local ecosystems. Natural disasters and the difficulty of feeding increasing populations both contributed to an atmosphere conducive to new ideas.

Population changes also played a significant impact in this shift. As human populations grew, so did the need for more effective methods of food production. While the hunter-gatherer lifestyle could support smaller societies, it could not support rapidly expanding ones. The search for reliable sources of nourishment drove the development of new survival techniques.

A New Way of Thinking About the Origins of Agriculture
The advent of agriculture represents a radical shift away from the nomadic, hunter-gatherer way of life that had previously prevailed. Early people began to intentionally manage their

surroundings for nourishment, rather than relying entirely on the immediate availability of wild resources. The domestication of animals and the raising of crops heralded the beginning of agriculture, a revolutionary development that would forever alter human civilization.

Evidence implies that ancient populations in the Middle Eastern Fertile Crescent were practicing purposeful agriculture as early as 10,000 BCE. Some of the earliest farmed crops included wheat, barley, and legumes, and some of the earliest domesticated animals included goats and sheep. This transition provided for a more reliable and regulated food supply, enabling towns to grow.

The Impact of Agriculture on Sedentary Culture and Society
The development of permanent settlements is a striking result of the agricultural revolution. Agricultural communities, in contrast to nomadic hunter-gatherer cultures, were able to settle down and farm their land and raise tamed animals. People's need to migrate in pursuit of resources declined after they learned to create extra food. This newfound peace allowed for the growth of settlements that would one day become towns and cities.

Social systems were drastically altered by the move to permanently inhabited areas. By putting away extra food, people gained a longer term sense of ownership over their assets. As some people became more prosperous and powerful than others, societal hierarchies emerged to reflect this unequal distribution of resources. The surplus also made possible the rise to power of experts who did not work in the food production sector, such as artisans, religious leaders, and monarchs.

The Urbanization of a Growing Population
As a result of agriculture, not only were more people able to survive, but human communities were able to expand at an unparalleled rate. Agriculture's consistent and ample food supply facilitated population growth by allowing cities to accommodate new residents. Cities grew from towns, which grew from settlements, as people increased.

Human society underwent radical transformation as a result of urbanization, a defining feature of the Agricultural Revolution. Settlements grew become economic, cultural, and creative powerhouses. People in cities were able to more easily trade products, information, and services with one another, which accelerated the progress of civilizations. Agriculture, population growth, and urbanization all worked together to fuel human society's growth in complexity and variety.

Changes in the Surplus and Trade in the Economic System
Communities' urgent food needs were addressed and excess food production was created thanks to agriculture. This surplus was a stimulus for economic revolutions, as cultures could now store excess resources for times of scarcity or exchange them with other communities. Intricate commerce networks were fueled by the possibility of trading agricultural surpluses.
Ancient landscapes were crisscrossed by trade routes that linked areas that produced diverse goods. Cultures were

enriched as a result of increased communication and the spread of new technologies as a result of economic integration. The excess paved the way for diversification of economies through the specialization of labor, with people devoting themselves to fields like trade, administration, and the arts.

Developments in Technology
Innovations in science and engineering were sparked by the need to improve agricultural practices. Plows, irrigation systems, and better seed selection all arose as a result of the demand for more effective agricultural techniques and tools. These innovations boosted agricultural output, which in turn allowed cultures to support greater populations and set the stage for the development of more intricate social systems.

The surplus allowed nations to invest in a wide range of technologies, not just agricultural implements. The arts of pottery making, metalworking, and building rose to prominence, elevating people's standard of living. The advances of later civilizations can be traced back to the accumulated knowledge about farming methods and technical developments that served as a foundation for further scientific progress in several sectors.

Changes in Society and Culture
The cultural and social repercussions of the transition from hunter-gatherer to sedentary farming cultures were far-reaching. The accumulation of riches and things made possible by the sedentary lifestyle allowed for the growth of

sophisticated social institutions. The development of surplus made it possible to fund non-agricultural specialists, which in turn led to the institutionalization of caste and other forms of social stratification.

Even religious ideas changed over time. Many agricultural communities developed to equate gods with the sun, rain, and fertility that were essential to their way of life. The cultural identity of these communities was shaped by the rituals and ceremonies that were connected with the cyclical rhythm of agricultural seasons. Due to the need for a consistent and well-defined growing space, the idea of land ownership rose to prominence, and property rights and geographic borders were formally established.

Problems and Environmental Repercussions
Although it resulted in extraordinary improvements, the Agricultural Revolution was not without its share of difficulties and environmental impacts. Deforestation, caused by humans making room for farmland, has altered ecosystems and reduced biodiversity. Monoculture farming practices accelerated soil degradation and erosion. Some ecosystems were altered to the point of overgrazing because of the domestication of animals for agricultural purposes.

The interconnectedness between human societies and the natural world is illustrated by these environmental repercussions. As humans have learned to mold and manage their surroundings to suit their purposes, they have also assumed the obligation to lessen the disruption their actions cause to natural systems. The difficulties in farming highlight the complex interdependencies among people, machines, and nature.

Conclusion

Finally, the investigation of the transition from hunter-gatherer groups to settled agricultural communities reveals a rich tapestry of interwoven factors that impacted human history. The shift from nomadic subsistence living to agricultural communities has far-reaching effects on many facets of human life, from economic systems to cultural norms.

The Agricultural Revolution was not a solitary event but a lengthy and diverse process that developed over millennia. It catapulted humankind into an age of innovation, population increase, and urbanization, setting the stage for the emergence of sophisticated societies. Nonetheless, it also ushered in environmental issues that reverberate in the present day, stressing the importance of maintaining a healthy equilibrium between human cultures and the natural world.

The roots of modern civilization and the difficulties inherent in advancement can be better understood by delving into the nuances of this transition. We may learn a lot about the strength and flexibility of human societies by thinking about their development from hunter-gathering to agrarian communities. Human ingenuity, environmental factors, and the ever-shifting fabric of human civilization all played a part in the Agricultural Revolution.

- **Examination of key developments such as the domestication of plants and animals**

  The domestication of plants and animals is a watershed moment in the history of human societies because it exemplifies the inventiveness and resourcefulness of humans. One of the most notable aspects of the Agricultural Revolution was the complex process of deliberately cultivating plants and taming animals for human use. Domesticating plants and animals was a pivotal historical moment that paved the way for permanent agricultural settlements, and we'll look into the major events surrounding this topic.

  The Transformation of Plants into Domesticated Crops
  Origins of Agriculture in the Fertile Crescent: The cradle of agriculture, located in the Fertile Crescent, witnessed the initial trials in plant domestication circa 10,000 BCE. Wild grasses were domesticated to produce einkorn, emmer, and barley as ancient populations in the area ranging from modern-day Iraq to Israel made the shift from nomadic to settled agriculture. These pioneers in agriculture foresaw the benefits of selecting and planting seeds from plants with favorable qualities, setting in motion a chain of events that eventually resulted in the creation of food staples.

  Plants were domesticated through a process of selective breeding and seed cultivation. Farmers back in the day saw that different wild plants had different qualities and started picking seeds from the ones with the best ones, such bigger seeds, pest resistance, and the ability to thrive in their particular climate. The application of this selective pressure over many generations allowed for the evolution of domesticated cultivars with enhanced viability in the field.

Crop diversity increased when agriculture extended to new areas and new types of crops were domesticated to suit local climates and human requirements. In East Asia, rice became a staple food, whereas in Mesoamerica and the Andes, corn and potatoes did the same. Human groups interacted with their environments in complex ways throughout the domestication process, producing a diverse and abundant variety of domesticated plants.

deep Implications for Human Nutrition and Social Progress
The domestication of plants had deep implications for human nutrition and social progress. More people could be fed since food was more consistent and plentiful thanks to agriculture. Human food habits changed drastically as they shifted from relying on a wide range of foraged plants to relying on only a few of staple crops. Consequences of this shift were mixed, as it helped greater populations be sustained but also led to a possible decline in food diversity.

Animal Domestication: The Transformation of Wild Creatures into Tame Pets
Simultaneous with the domestication of plants, humans also started taming and breeding animals for use in diverse human activities. Again, the Fertile Crescent was an important location for the early domestication of animals. Sheep and goats were

among the first domesticated animals because they provided a reliable supply of food and fiber.

Animals were domesticated through a process of selective breeding in order to increase the prevalence of characteristics that would be useful to human communities. Animals that were tame, social, and willing to be kept as pets were prized for their utility to humans. As a result of careful breeding over many generations, new types of domesticated animals emerged, each with its own set of advantages and disadvantages.

Domesticated animals, like domesticated plants, have a wide range of species represented. Based on local requirements and available resources, various societies around the world have developed a specialization in particular species. Cattle and swine were the first animals to be domesticated in Eurasia, whereas llamas and alpacas were bred in the Americas for their wool and as pack animals. The ability of human societies to adjust to their settings is reflected in the wide variety of domesticated animals.

The domestication of animals greatly influenced farming and other forms of manual labor. Animals were domesticated for their labor in plowing fields, hauling commodities, and making materials like wool and leather. Animals were used into agricultural systems to improve productivity, which allowed for the cultivation of bigger plots of land.

Beyond their utilitarian value, domesticated animals also had significant social and cultural meaning. Certain animals also had religious or ceremonial significance in some societies, and they became emblems of wealth and prestige. Early agricultural cultures were shaped by the interdependence that developed between people and their tamed animals.

The Relationship Between the Domestication of Plants and Animals

Domestication of plants and animals did not happen separately but frequently in combination, resulting in symbiotic interactions between them. Livestock dung was essential in many agricultural systems because it fertilized fields, and crop leftovers were used as animal feed. The interconnected nature of these early farming communities increased the longevity of their agricultural methods and boosted their overall output.

Changes in Population Distribution:

The domestication of plants and animals dramatically altered settlement patterns. Care for domesticated animals and crops led to the growth of permanent communities. Towns and villages sprang up as the nerve centers of the agricultural revolution, paving the way for the emergence of sophisticated societies with their own economic, social, and cultural systems.

Problems and New Approaches to Domestication:

Animal domestication had its own set of difficulties. Unlike plants, animals could still move around and even resisted being caged in some circumstances. In-depth knowledge of animal behavior and selective breeding to eliminate untamed features were essential to overcoming these obstacles. Domesticating animals usually involved plenty of trial and error and a nuanced knowledge of the species involved.

The proximity of humans and domesticated animals allowed for the spread of illness between them. This contributed to genetic bottlenecks. Early agricultural cultures faced formidable obstacles due to the advent of zoonotic diseases. There was a loss of genetic diversity in domesticated populations due to bottlenecks that occurred throughout the domestication process, rendering them more susceptible to illnesses and environmental shifts.

Effects on Human Cultures:
The domestication of plants and animals was crucial to the maintenance of expanding human populations and the development of urban centers. Increased population densities and larger settlements resulted from the availability of sufficient food supplies. The urbanization that defined complex societies was propelled by the interplay of agriculture and population increase.

Domesticating plants and animals triggered significant changes to the economy. The ability to produce surplus food and harness animal labor both had a role in the economic diversity of societies. As communities began to generate surplus food and goods, it became possible for individuals to specialize in agriculture, commerce, and other fields. The establishment of complex economic systems and the growth of markets was made possible by this economic diversification.

Developments in technology were stimulated by the domestication of plants and animals. Plows and yokes, among other agricultural implements, were designed to make farmers' lives easier. Technology improvements were also made in the areas of animal husbandry, selective breeding, and food processing. In addition to boosting agricultural output, these breakthroughs laid the door for developments in many other areas.

Changes in Society and Culture:
The transition from nomadic hunter-gatherer lifestyles to sedentary agricultural societies resulted in substantial alterations to social systems. The development of agriculture and animal domestication paved the way for long-term settlements, which in turn fueled the expansion of smaller communities into larger ones, and ultimately into cities. As a result of this shift, sophisticated social hierarchies emerged, with leaders, artisans, and religious figures all playing significant roles.

Domestication of plants and animals had an impact on cultural behaviors and belief systems. The cyclical character of agricultural seasons got linked with religious rituals and celebrations. Domestic and wild animals both often served as symbols in folktales and legends across the world. The cultural identity of early agricultural cultures was shaped by folklore, mythology, and religious beliefs that reflected the strong interaction between humans and animals.

There was an effect on gender roles as a result of the agricultural revolution. As communities began to form, people began to develop expertise in specific fields. Planting and caring for crops were traditionally seen as women's work in early agriculture. Gender-specific roles emerged as a result of the increased labor needs of agriculture.

The Long-Term Effects on the Environment:
Altering Ecosystems: The domestication of plants and animals has a tremendous impact on ecosystems. Deforestation and other changes in biodiversity can be traced back to the domestication of previously forested areas. Some natural plant and animal species were lost when humans introduced domesticated species. Unintentionally, agricultural activities led to widespread environmental disruption.

Problems with Long-Term Sustainability Conventional farming relied on a careful balancing act between human activity and the natural environment to be successful in the early days. Threats to long-term viability were presented by methods like monoculture and overgrazing. Understanding the significance of responsible land management in the pursuit of sustainable agriculture is essential in light of the long-term effects of these activities on soil fertility and ecosystem health.

Conclusion

Key breakthroughs in the domestication of plants and animals, when examined in detail, indicate a complex interplay between human creativity, environmental dynamics, and society change. Settled agricultural communities, urbanization, and the creation of complex civilizations can be traced back to the intentional cultivation of plants and the taming of animals.

Domestication of plants and animals was not a static or uniform process that occurred over centuries or even millennia, but rather a dynamic and context-dependent event. Symbiotic interactions between humans, plants, and animals were cultivated, and in-depth knowledge of natural processes was required. Both deliberate and unintended, these activities have far-reaching effects on human history and continue to have an impact on modern communities.

The domestication of plants and animals has had far-reaching consequences, which must be taken into account when thinking about this topic. The domestication of plants and animals profoundly altered human life, providing a steady food source that allowed for population increase and laying the framework for complex society. But it also brought problems like disease spread, genetic bottlenecks, and environmental damage, bringing into sharp focus the delicate equilibrium that exists between human actions and the natural world.

Insightful into the origins of agriculture, the intricacies of early human cultures, and the ongoing challenges and opportunities of contemporary agricultural practices, understanding the main developments in the domestication of plants and animals is essential. Crops cultivated, animals raised, and complex relationships with the natural environment all carry on the legacy of domestication.

- **Impact on social structures, technology, and human civilization**

  Agriculture was a watershed moment in human history, one that led to profound societal changes, rapid scientific developments, and the emergence of advanced civilizations. Every aspect of human life was altered by the transition from nomadic hunter-gatherer societies to agricultural settlements. Here we investigate agriculture's far-reaching effects on human society, technical progress, and the development of culture as a whole.

  Consequences for Social Orders:
  The shift from nomadic hunter-gatherer cultures to sedentary farming communities paved the way for the formation of sophisticated social institutions. Villages, towns, and finally cities blossomed as a result of the capacity to cultivate crops and domesticate animals, allowing for permanent settlements. A departure from the relative simplicity of nomadic lifestyles, these urban settlements became the sites of cultural exchange, economic activity, and governance.

  The transition to settled agriculture brought about the creation of social hierarchies as a result of the amassing of excess resources and the establishment of permanent settlements. Social stratification developed as certain people amassed money and power through the ownership of land, access to resources, or the possession of unique talents. Early agricultural civilizations became stratified due in part to the incorporation of leaders, artisans, and religious figures into the social fabric.

Agriculture paved the way for the development of new fields of endeavor and the division of labor within communities. As surplus food production became possible, individuals could participate in vocations beyond immediate subsistence demands. As a result, people began to specialize in different areas, such as agriculture, commerce, craftsmanship, administration, and so on. The complexity of social systems can be traced back to the interdependence of various roles.

The transition to agriculture affected gender roles and the structure of families. As tasks became increasingly specialized, gender-specific positions arose. Planting and caring for crops were traditionally seen as women's work in early agriculture. Agriculture's growing labor needs prompted the establishment of clear gender roles within households and communities.

Inheritance and property rights grew in importance as agricultural societies institutionalized established communities and the idea of private landownership. Land, a necessary component for agricultural production, eventually grew to be a status symbol. Wealth and landownership passed down through families, contributing to the creation of hereditary social classes, which in turn helped to perpetuate social hierarchies.

Religious and Cultural Institutions: Agricultural practices shaped religious and cultural institutions. The cyclical character of agricultural seasons got linked with religious rituals and celebrations. The early agricultural societies' pantheons became more dominated by fertility, harvest, and agricultural process deities. Temples and other places of worship were the spiritual and political centerpieces of these societies.

Technology's Reaction:
Innovations in Farming Equipment Innovations in farming equipment were sparked by the demand for more effective farming techniques. Plows, hoes, and sickles replaced simple digging sticks as the primary agricultural tools. The increased efficiency of cultivation made possible by these technologies allowed farmers to till more land, hence raising agricultural output. The creation of these instruments paved the way for subsequent technical advances.

The need for irrigation systems arose from the necessity of growing crops in regions with an unreliable supply of water. To regulate the delivery of water to farms, early civilizations built canals, channels, and other forms of irrigation infrastructure. This breakthrough made it possible to farm in arid regions and brought farming to places that had previously been unsuitable for it.

Domesticating animals for agricultural purposes required the practice of selective breeding to produce offspring with desirable characteristics. This method resulted in the creation of domesticated breeds optimized for certain tasks including plowing, transporting, and milk/wool production. Early forms of biotechnology involved the selective breeding and animal husbandry techniques that facilitated the alteration of the genetic makeup of domesticated species.

Because of the overabundance of agricultural output, it was necessary to develop efficient methods of storing and preserving food. In order to safeguard their food supply and keep away pests, early agricultural cultures created grain storage technologies including granaries and silos. Drying, smoking, and fermenting were used to preserve foods for longer, which helped people get through drought and famine.

Metallurgy and Craftsmanship: The surplus from agriculture allowed for the growth of these industries. Plows, axes, and sickles, all made of metal, quickly became indispensable in the agricultural industry. Better and longer lasting tools could be made because to the development of metallurgy, which increased productivity in farming and other fields.

The development of permanent communities and the building of long-lasting structures called for improvements in building technology. Construction techniques using mud bricks and stone allowed early agrarian communities to establish stronger and more complex buildings. These communities' scientific prowess was on display in the granaries, storage facilities, and, later on, colossal buildings they erected.

Consequences for Humanity's Culture:
One of the defining effects of agriculture on human civilization was the ability to maintain bigger people, which facilitated the emergence of urban centers. Increased population densities and larger settlements were possible because of agriculture's

consistent and plentiful food supply. Population growth spurred urbanization, which in turn defined sophisticated societies.

In terms of economic shifts, agriculture was essential in establishing new institutional norms and encouraging greater economic diversity. Specialized roles and occupations emerged as a result of the surplus food supply and the capacity to harness animal labor. Trade, markets, and the growth of wealth beyond basic necessities were all made possible by this economic diversification.

The surplus in agricultural output allowed for the establishment of trade networks that linked previously isolated areas, resulting in increased opportunities for cultural exchange. Communities were more likely to interact with one another and share ideas and practices when they traded excess agricultural products and other items and technologies. Cross-continental trade helped spread new ideas, words, and customs from one place to the next.

The abundance of crops allowed for investments in research and development, advancing both science and technology. Improvements in agriculture, such new equipment and irrigation systems, were met with developments in other industries. Mathematical principles for land measuring, agricultural season calendars, and astronomical observations tied to planting and harvesting cycles were established by early agricultural societies.

The agricultural stability that allowed for the development of sophisticated cultural practices and forms of creative expression. With stable populations and an abundance of resources, cultures could devote more time and energy to developing their artistic, literary, and architectural traditions. These civilizations' cultural vitality was reflected in their monumental architecture, exquisite pottery, and creative depictions of rural life.

Politics and Administrative Structures:
More intricate forms of government were required when established communities and surplus-based economies emerged. Political systems emerged to handle the affairs of rising populations, including the administration of justice, resource allocation, and defense. Agricultural societies' administration was greatly aided by the development of leadership positions, rulership, and administrative structures.

Impact on the Environment and Long-Term Sustainability:
Agriculture relied on a stable relationship between humans and their natural surroundings. Deforestation, monoculture, and overgrazing were all practices that undermined sustainability. The environmental impacts of early agricultural societies' actions prompted ongoing debates regarding land conservation and sustainable farming.

Problems and Criticisms
Although agriculture led to previously unimaginable improvements, it also had far-reaching negative effects on the environment. The clearing of land for cultivation led to

deforestation, altering ecosystems and impacting biodiversity. Monoculture farming practices accelerated soil degradation and erosion. Changing ecosystems and even overgrazing in some areas are direct results of the domestication of animals for agricultural purposes.

The surplus produced by agriculture helped foster the growth of social stratification and inequality. Land ownership solidified class disparities as a means to amass money and influence. As a result of the division of labor, some social roles became more highly valued than others. Early agrarian cultures were riven by these kinds of ingrained inequalities.

Infectious Disease Spreading Close contact between humans and domesticated animals has led to the emergence of zoonotic diseases. The concentration of humans and animals in agricultural settings made for ideal conditions for the spread of illness. The urgency of improving public health procedures was highlighted by this difficulty.

Conclusion:
In conclusion, the story of agriculture and its influence on human society, technology, and culture is complicated and multi-layered, spanning many centuries. The transition from nomadic to agricultural societies was a watershed moment in human history, ushering in a period of unprecedented cultural and scientific advancement.

Because of the opportunities and difficulties given by agriculture, human communities adapted by developing hierarchies, specialization, and division of labor. The foundation for future development was created by technological innovations such as agricultural tools and irrigation systems. The broad trajectory of human civilization, driven by the agricultural revolution, witnessed the growth of urban centers, economic diversity, and the flowering of artistic and scientific endeavors.

This life-altering trip did not come without its share of difficulties and repercussions, however. Human cultures have complicated relationships with the natural world, as evidenced by environmental consequences, social disparities, and the spread of disease. Understanding the complex relationship between development, sustainability, and humanity's continued progress is crucial when contemplating agriculture's legacy. Agriculture's history is more than simply a story; it's a conversation that defines how humans interact with nature, technology, and each other.

Chapter 2: The Renaissance and the Age of Discovery

Overview of the Renaissance as a cultural and intellectual revival

The Renaissance, a period lasting roughly from the 14th to the 17th century, stands as a significant epoch in human history, marked by an incredible resurgence of cultural, intellectual, and creative achievements. It was during the Renaissance when interest in classical learning, humanism, and artistic experimentation were revitalized after languishing during the dark ages of the Middle Ages. The many facets of the Renaissance are examined in this survey, from the cultural and intellectual renaissance it sparked to the lasting influence it has left on the development of human civilization.

Setting and History:
The Middle Ages were followed by the Renaissance, which developed as a reaction to the feudalism, scholasticism, and religious dogmatism of the era before it. Optimism and exploration were in the air as Europe began to recover from the traumas of the Black Death and the Hundred Years' War. The seeds of the Renaissance were planted during this time of change.

The Renaissance was characterized by the rediscovery and subsequent resurrection of classical knowledge from antiquity, particularly that of ancient Greece and Rome. The rediscovery of ancient manuscripts, hidden away for centuries in monastic libraries, sparked a newfound appreciation for the ideas of Aristotle, Plato, and Cicero. This return to classical learning paved the way for the humanist movement, which placed a premium on the worth of individual experience, rational thought, and creative expression.

Humanism, the Renaissance's Central Concept:
The ideology of humanism was crucial to the Renaissance because it lauded the worth of the individual, the possibilities of humanity, and the quest for knowledge. To promote a more complete worldview that integrated religious faith with a genuine appreciation for human achievement, humanists tried to reconcile Christian teachings with the wisdom of classical antiquity.

Grammar, rhetoric, history, poetry, and moral philosophy were all included in the Studia Humanitatis, a curriculum pushed for by humanist scholars. The goal of this method of instruction was to produce a person who was well-versed in both the classics and the modern world. Humanist education came to place a premium on oratory, analysis, and a holistic view of the human condition.

The Perfect Renaissance Man: The "Renaissance man" idealized in humanist thought was a polymath who was well-versed in many disciplines. Leonardo da Vinci is a classic example of this type because he was a multi-talented genius who excelled in many fields. The quest of knowledge became not merely a scholastic undertaking but a way of life, emphasizing the boundless potential of the human mind.

Revival of the Arts:

A profound shift occurred in the way art was expressed during the Renaissance. Artists abandoned the medieval period's ornate, symbolic style for one that was more naturalistic and focused on the human figure. Artists began to place a premium on realism, perspective, and the anatomical correctness of the human figure.

A pantheon of artistic masters emerged during the Renaissance, all of whom aided in the period's overall flowering of creative talent. The peaks of Renaissance art can be seen in works like Leonardo da Vinci's "Mona Lisa" and "The Last Supper," Michelangelo's "David" and "Sistine Chapel," and Raphael's "Frescoes" in the Vatican. These artists, who were frequently commissioned by affluent patrons and religious institutions, produced works that perfectly encapsulated the spirit of their day.

Technique Developments During the Renaissance, artists explored new approaches to traditional practices like linear perspective, chiaroscuro (the use of light and shadow), and sfumato (the blurring or softening of lines). These developments not only altered the visual arts, but also altered people's perspectives and methods of interacting with the environment.

Reformation in Literature:

Classical literature was given new life by Renaissance scholars who hoped to bring it to a wider audience. Key to spreading classical texts and encouraging a culture of literacy, Johannes Gutenberg's creation of the printing press in the mid-15th century. The widespread dissemination of printed books sparked a cultural and intellectual revolution in Europe.

The part of Humanist Literature: Humanist academics, like Petrarch and Erasmus, played a vital part in establishing the literary environment of the Renaissance. Their compositions, which were frequently composed in the vernacular, praised the elegance of language and the diversity of human speech. Poetry by Petrarch and "In Praise of Folly" by Erasmus are two examples of the humanist emphasis on eloquence, reason, and the investigation of human nature.

The Renaissance saw the creation of epic literary works that drew inspiration from classical texts, marking the beginning of the modern epic. Medieval allegory and Renaissance humanism come together in Dante Alighieri's "The Divine Comedy," an epic poem that charts the soul's journey through Purgatory, Hell, and finally, Paradise. Just as "The Faerie Queene" by Edmund Spenser, a poet of the English Renaissance, embodied the ideals of chivalry and virtue, it reflected the traditions of classical epic poetry.

Revival of Science:
During the Renaissance, scholars shifted their focus from ancient authority to empirical and observational methods of inquiry, marking a watershed moment in the history of science. The Scientific Revolution of the succeeding centuries had its roots in the Scientific Renaissance.

Scientists of the Renaissance period made significant contributions, including Nicolaus Copernicus (whose heliocentric model challenged geocentric ideas of the cosmos) and Johannes Kepler (who defined the laws of planetary motion). In questioning the prevalent Aristotelian notions, Galileo Galilei's telescopic observations and experiments ushered in a new era of scientific investigation.

Affect on Culture:
The Renaissance ushered in a period of great social change, one that shook up convention and encouraged a thirst for knowledge. Increased access to education has led to a more educated and informed populace, which in turn has led to a more open exchange of ideas and a more progressive culture.

The Power of Patronage: The Renaissance would not have been possible without the financial backing of wealthy patrons like the Medici family of Florence. Their support allowed artists, academics, and scientists of the time to pursue their passions, resulting in a flourishing of the arts and sciences.

Legacy of Culture: The Renaissance left a legacy of culture that is still shaping the globe today. The period's scientific discoveries, literary classics, and artistic achievements all set the stage for the growth of modern Western civilization.

Humanism's Enduring Impact: The humanist concept that fueled the Renaissance continues to resonate in contemporary thought. The contemporary world's cultural and intellectual legacy is indelibly marked by the values of respect for the individual, the quest for knowledge, and the celebration of human creativity.

Empiricism and the Scientific Method: The Scientific Renaissance is often credited with laying the groundwork for the scientific revolution that followed. The trajectory of humankind's rethinking of its understanding of the natural world was put in motion by the concepts of inquiry, experimentation, and evidence-based reasoning.

Conclusion:

In sum, the Renaissance is an intellectual and cultural renaissance that altered the trajectory of human history. The Renaissance was a period of great cultural flowering, artistic invention, and scientific investigation that emerged from the transitional period between the medieval and modern periods. Collectively, the renaissance of classical learning, humanist thought, and the growth of the arts and sciences altered the very foundations of society.

The Renaissance was not a passing phase in human history, but rather a potent and persistent influence that is still felt in today's ideas and culture. Art, literature, and science that have stood the test of time because of it have left an indelible mark on subsequent generations. The Renaissance is a symbol of the transformational power of ideas and a monument to the limitless possibilities of human ingenuity and inquiry.

Exploration of the Age of Discovery and major expeditions

Between the 15th and 17th centuries, an era known as the Age of Discovery saw tremendous marine exploration and expansion. European powers were spurred to action by a confluence of economic, political, religious, and technological developments, which they used to transform the map of the world. In this investigation, we look into the great expeditions of the Age of Discovery, analyzing the leading explorers, their motivations, and the global impact of their travels.

Exploration Motivators:
Financial considerations ranked high on the list of exploration's key motivators. To avoid the Ottoman Empire's monopoly on the old overland routes, European nations looked for alternative ways to Asia's wealthy markets. Alternative maritime routes were sought after because of the high demand for spices, silks, and precious metals.

Technical Developments: Long-distance maritime travel was greatly aided by developments in navigational technology. Sailors were able to pinpoint their location with more accuracy after the invention of the astrolabe, quadrant, and refined navigational charts. The exploration possibilities of ships were greatly improved with the advent of the caravel.

Exploration and the spread of Christianity to other regions were both driven by religious fervor and missionary impulses on the part of European rulers. Explorators saw their journeys as a chance to convert non-Christians and spread the authority of the Catholic Church after the Reconquista in Spain and the expulsion of Jews and Muslims.

Exploration was also motivated by a desire for political and cultural hegemony. European countries, especially Spain and Portugal, vied for worldwide dominance. Control over trade routes, colonies, and the acquisition of precious resources were viewed as crucial parts of national prestige and power.

Significant Voyages and Their Navigators:
Cristobal Colón (1492-1502):
Christopher Columbus, with Spanish support, set sail in 1492 for a westward journey across the world to Asia. Instead, he arrived at the Caribbean islands, paving the way for future European exploration and settlement in the New World. Columbus made four trips over the Atlantic Ocean, opening up trade between Europe and the Americas.

Vasco da Gama, a Portuguese explorer, set sail in 1497 to establish a water path to Asia. He didn't return until 1499. His group was the first to sail around Africa's Cape of Good Hope, allowing them easy access to India's opulent spice trade. This accomplishment greatly impacted international trade by reducing the importance of more conventional overland routes.

Magellan, Ferdinand (1519–1522)
Ferdinand Magellan led the first mission to round the globe, which was funded by Spain. Magellan did not make it to the

end of the expedition, but his fleet, led by Juan Sebastián Elcano, successfully circumnavigated the globe. This enormous feat illustrated the size of our planet and the possibilities for worldwide travel.

Italian explorer John Cabot (1497) is credited with discovering areas of North America, including the coast of Newfoundland, while sailing under the flag of the English crown. In doing so, he paved the way for future English claims in the New World.

Amerigo Vespucci (1499–1502) was an Italian explorer whose expeditions helped confirm that the territories explored by Christopher Columbus belonged to a new continent. His contribution to the understanding of continental separation is reflected in the fact that the continent we now call America was given its name after him.

The Spanish expedition headed by Hernán Cortés (1519–1521) that ultimately conquered the Aztec Empire in what is now Mexico. His conquest was a watershed moment in the history of European colonization of the Americas; it brought enormous wealth to Spain and laid the groundwork for even greater Spanish development in the region.

Conquering the Inca Empire in what is now Peru was an expedition led by another Spanish conquistador, Francisco Pizarro (1532–1533). Pizarro's achievement contributed to the influx of wealth into Spain, underlining the economic prospects that exploration and colonization afforded.

Changes Caused by Exploration:

Columbian interchange: The Columbian Exchange, a revolutionary process of global biological interchange between the Old World and the New World, was launched during the Age of Discovery. Changes in agriculture, population, and ecosystems resulted from the movement of plants, animals, and diseases between continents. In the Old World, many people relied on crops like potatoes, tomatoes, and maize, while in the New World, the introduction of horses, livestock, and diseases like smallpox had a profound effect.

Exploration of the Americas, Africa, and Asia by Europeans led to the colonization of enormous areas of those continents and its subsequent exploitation. Colonies were set up by European countries so that they could mine them for commodities like gold, spices, and food. Both the colonizers and the colonized were affected significantly by the social, economic, and cultural outcomes of this colonialism.

Cultural spread: Exploration encouraged cultural spread as individuals from different regions of the world came into contact. Global cultures benefited from the sharing of ideas, languages, religions, and technology. Cultures clashed and adapted to new circumstances, but this often led to disputes and power struggles.

The opening of new sea routes had a profound effect on international trade. Vasco da Gama's discovery of a sea route to Asia cut through territory held by the Ottoman Empire. The

Silk Road's economic importance waned as sea trade gained ground as a result of this shift.

Exploration aided in the spread of new technology to previously undiscovered civilizations. The Europeans influenced the development of new ship types, navigational tools, and weaponry. Papermaking, printing, and gunpowder all made their way to Europe from Asia at the same time.

The wealth brought back from the colonies helped fuel an economic boom in Europe. The trade of precious metals, spices, and other luxury items fueled the expansion of the Spanish and Portuguese empires. This economic growth paved the way for the establishment of modern European nations.

Difficulties and Debate:
Mistreatment of Indigenous Peoples During Colonialism Exploitation, forced labor, and persecution were commonplace during the colonial period. The European powers were responsible for the degradation of local economies and ecosystems through their resource extraction activities. New diseases, mass migration, and the loss of indigenous languages and cultural practices were just some of colonization's socioeconomic and cultural costs.

Wars broke out between the expanding European powers and the preexisting populations and civilizations. Attempts to defy imperial rule can be seen in historical resistance movements like the Aztec and Inca uprisings against Spanish colonization. Numerous wars broke out in the colonized areas, and the history of those places was profoundly affected by the clash of cultures and the imposition of European systems of rule.

Native American and other indigenous communities experienced significant upheaval as a result of European colonization. Diseases carried by explorers, often unknowingly, wiped off entire populations. Traditional patterns of living were drastically altered as European economic and social institutions were imposed.

Conclusion:
The Age of Discovery was a watershed moment in human history, characterized by the boldness of explorers, the meeting of disparate cultures, and the reshaping of the world's topography. Initiating the Columbian Exchange and redrawing the globe, the great expeditions of this time period established the basis for today's globalized society. Exploration leaves an indelible mark on the fabric of cultures around the world, both positively and negatively, and so influences the development of human history for generations to come. Understanding the interdependence of human civilizations is inextricably tied to the Age of Discovery, and it is crucial that we recognize the intricacies of this historical chapter as we look back on its successes, problems, and enduring legacies.

- **Discussion of the impact of new knowledge and global exploration on society**

    When the Age of Discovery began, it ushered in a period of unprecedented global exploration and the unrelenting pursuit of new knowledge. As European nations embarked on adventurous excursions to faraway regions, the acquisition of fresh insights, technologies, and resources had enormous effects for cultures across the globe. In this all-encompassing analysis, we look at how advances in knowledge and global travel have altered society from a variety of angles, including the cultural, economic, technological, and social.

    Changing Economic Conditions:
    One of the most noticeable and long-lasting results of global discovery was the realignment of trade routes throughout the world. Direct sea routes to Asia were established, mostly by Vasco da Gama and Christopher Columbus, which allowed them to avoid the Ottoman Empire's control over the more conventional overland routes. This shift in trade patterns generated both possibilities and threats for economies around the world.

    Colonization of the Americas, Africa, and Asia became a cornerstone of economic revolutions throughout this time, giving rise to colonial economies and mercantilism. Mercantilism developed as European countries tried to profit from the abundant resources of their colonies. The primary goal of colonial economies was to support European industrialization by providing essential raw resources.

Especially in Spain and Portugal, the colonial capture of precious metals, spices, and other rich resources led to a monetary windfall for Europe. This wealth was crucial in supporting future expeditions, propelling the rise of strong nation-states, and reshaping Africa's economic landscape.

The economic adjustments caused by global exploration contributed to capitalism's growth and maturation. Trade expansion, the rise of joint-stock businesses, and capital accumulation all played a role in the development of modern economic systems. This paved the way for the decline of feudalism and rise of capitalism in many European civilizations.

Impact of Cross-Cultural Contacts on Society
Cultural diffusion: the significant interchange of ideas, languages, religions, and technologies between diverse cultures that resulted from contact during global expansion. As different cultures borrowed from and borrowed from one another, it had a tremendous effect on those involved. New beliefs, practices, and customs emerged as a result of the mingling of various cultural traditions.

Explorers, merchants, and native peoples all had to communicate with one another because of their interactions. This resulted in the spread of new languages, with European languages becoming de facto lingua francas in many areas once under colonial rule. A new era of international communication and cultural exchange was ushered in as a result of the convergence of languages.

Religious Shifts: Exploration of the world was fueled in large part by a search for religious truth, and the resulting exposure to other faiths and practices radically altered the landscape of human spirituality. Missionary operations tried to introduce Christianity to new countries, leading to the conversion of indigenous populations. Explorers' religious views were both tested and enriched by their encounters with novel tenets of belief and ritual.

The flood of new information, artifacts, and cultural viewpoints from all over the world sparked an intellectual and artistic renaissance. Thinkers in Europe, bolstered by their exposure to the classics and the wealth of world experience, questioned long-held dogmas and ushered in a period of inquisitiveness. The Renaissance is a prime example of the flourishing of artistic expression and the cultural vitality of the period.

Developments in technology and the scientific revolution:
The difficulties encountered throughout global exploration generated major developments in navigational technology. Accurate sea travel became possible with the advent of tools like the astrolabe, quadrant, and upgraded navigational charts. The caravel's ability to adapt and navigate was important in enabling long-distance travel.

Exploration paved the way for the Scientific Revolution by generating empirical observations and technological advancements. Copernicus, Kepler, and Galileo were just a few of the intellectuals that pushed back against previously held ideas about the cosmos. The results of the Scientific Revolution opened the path for the contemporary scientific method and radically altered people's perspectives on the natural world.

Exploration aided in the spread of new technology between civilizations. The Europeans influenced the development of new ship types, navigational tools, and weaponry. Papermaking, printing, and gunpowder all had their genesis in Asia, but eventually made their way to Europe. The technological progress of the time can be attributed in part to this cross-cultural interaction.

Changes in Society and the Population:
Population Shifts and Migrations: Contacts between civilizations triggered migrations and demographic changes. The Columbian Exchange, for instance, facilitated the spread of flora, fauna, and pathogens from the Old World to the New. The population of Europe increased while that of the Americas was nearly wiped out as a result of this trade.

Exploration's impact on the economy paved the way for the development of social stratification. The colonial exploitation of indigenous peoples and the amassing of wealth from abroad trade led to the establishment of merchant classes. The social structures of European societies were profoundly affected by this stratification.

Tensions and confrontations arose frequently as a result of the cultural interactions between explorers, colonizers, and indigenous peoples. Interactions were complicated by linguistic, religious, and cultural differences. History in colonized areas was molded by both cooperation and resistance, triggered by the collision of cultures and the imposition of European norms.

The entrance of Europeans had a profound effect on indigenous communities, causing widespread upheaval. Smallpox and other foreign illnesses decimated native populations shortly after their arrival. The cultural shifts that resulted from the imposition of European economic and social systems were not limited to the formal institutions of society.

Difficulties and Debate:
Exploitation, forced labor, and persecution of native peoples were commonplace during the era of European discovery and colonization of the Americas. The European powers were responsible for the degradation of local economies and ecosystems through their resource extraction activities. New diseases, mass migration, and the loss of indigenous languages and cultural practices were just some of colonization's socioeconomic and cultural costs.

Wars broke out between the expanding European powers and the preexisting populations and civilizations. Attempts to defy imperial rule can be seen in historical resistance movements like the Aztec and Inca uprisings against Spanish colonization. Numerous wars broke out in the colonized areas, and the history of those places was profoundly affected by the clash of cultures and the imposition of European systems of rule.

Ethical Considerations There has been on-going debate over the ethical implications of exploration and colonization. The morality, fairness, and treatment of native peoples remain under close scrutiny. Historians and scholars debate the moral weight of decisions made and events that transpired during this time period.

Conclusion:
In conclusion, the Age of Discovery was nothing short of revolutionary because of the influence of new knowledge and global exploration on civilization. The fabric of human society was altered as a result of changes in the economy, the spread of new ideas, the development of new technologies, and the emergence of new social structures. Dynamic cultural exchange, fueled by curiosity and the need to learn more, left an everlasting impression on people all over the world.

Challenges, conflicts, and ethical difficulties emerged alongside the Age of Discovery's unparalleled innovations and opportunities. Both the benefits of learning new things and the drawbacks of unbridled growth are part of this era's enduring legacy. Understanding the interconnectedness of human history is shaped in part by this formative epoch, therefore it's important to take note of the subtleties, value the lasting contributions, and scrutinize the ethical dimensions. The Age of Exploration offers a window into the complicated relationship between discovery and learning as well as the ripple effects of societal change.

- **Examination of key figures like Leonardo da Vinci, Christopher Columbus, and others**

  The pages of history are adorned with the indelible imprints of individuals whose contributions have transcended their lifetimes, shaping the course of human history and leaving an enduring legacy. Among the myriad of figures who have graced the annals of history, Leonardo da Vinci and Christopher Columbus stand as towering figures, each embodying the spirit of their respective ages. In this comprehensive examination, we delve into the lives, achievements, and impact of key figures from different spheres, unraveling the tapestry of their genius, vision, and influence on the world.

  Leonardo da Vinci: A Renaissance Polymath:
  Early Life and Education:
  Leonardo da Vinci, born on April 15, 1452, in Vinci, Italy, epitomizes the essence of the Renaissance polymath. His early life was marked by an insatiable curiosity and an inherent talent for the arts. Apprenticed to the renowned artist Andrea del Verrocchio in Florence, da Vinci honed his artistic skills, but his interests extended far beyond the canvas.

  Artistic Masterpieces:
  Leonardo da Vinci's artistic legacy is characterized by an unparalleled mastery of various art forms. His iconic works, including the "Mona Lisa" and "The Last Supper," exemplify his revolutionary approach to composition, perspective, and use of light and shadow. The meticulousness of his artistic

endeavors reflects a fusion of artistic brilliance and scientific inquiry.

Scientific Inquiry and Inventions:
Beyond his artistic pursuits, da Vinci's notebooks reveal an extraordinary scientific mind. His investigations spanned anatomy, engineering, mathematics, and natural sciences. Da Vinci's anatomical sketches, such as the Vitruvian Man, demonstrated his keen observations of the human body. Additionally, he conceptualized numerous inventions, from flying machines to war machines, showcasing a visionary approach to technological innovation.

Interdisciplinary Approach:
What sets Leonardo da Vinci apart is his pioneering interdisciplinary approach. He seamlessly blended art and science, seeing no boundaries between the two. Da Vinci's notebooks, filled with sketches, observations, and musings, serve as a testament to his belief that art and science were intertwined facets of understanding the natural world.

Legacy and Influence:
Leonardo da Vinci's influence extends far beyond his lifetime. His integration of artistic expression and scientific inquiry laid the foundation for future generations of polymaths. The Renaissance spirit of curiosity, creativity, and a holistic approach to knowledge owes much to the pioneering work of da Vinci. His legacy reverberates not only in the halls of art museums but also in the laboratories of scientists and the studios of inventors.

Christopher Columbus: The Explorer of New Horizons:

Early Life and Background:

Christopher Columbus, born in Genoa, Italy, around 1451, emerged as a central figure in the Age of Discovery. Raised in a family of modest means, Columbus embarked on a maritime career from an early age, acquiring the navigational skills that would later propel him into the annals of history.

Quest for a Western Route to Asia:

Columbus's most renowned endeavor was his quest for a western route to Asia. Inspired by a desire to establish direct trade routes to the lucrative markets of the East, Columbus sought the patronage of various European monarchs. After numerous rejections, he secured the support of Ferdinand and Isabella of Spain, setting the stage for his historic voyages.

Voyages of Discovery:

Columbus embarked on four voyages between 1492 and 1504, forever altering the map of the known world. His first journey, setting sail on August 3, 1492, led to the discovery of the Americas. The encounter with the islands of the Caribbean marked a pivotal moment in history, reshaping global trade routes and initiating an era of European exploration in the New World.

Impact on Global Exploration:

Christopher Columbus's voyages had profound consequences for global exploration. His encounters with the Americas opened the floodgates for further exploration and colonization by European powers. The Columbian Exchange, the transatlantic transfer of plants, animals, and cultures, initiated by Columbus's journeys, reshaped societies on both sides of the Atlantic.

Controversies and Critiques:

Columbus's legacy is not without controversy. While celebrated for his role in connecting the Old World and the New World, he is also critiqued for the negative impacts of European colonization, including the exploitation and mistreatment of indigenous populations. The complex legacy of Columbus is a subject of ongoing debate and reflection.

Other Key Figures:

Ferdinand Magellan (1480-1521):

Ferdinand Magellan, a Portuguese explorer in the service of Spain, led the first expedition to circumnavigate the globe. While Magellan did not survive the entire journey, his fleet completed the circumnavigation under the command of Juan Sebastián Elcano. This monumental achievement demonstrated the vastness of the Earth and the potential for global exploration.

Amerigo Vespucci (1454-1512):

Amerigo Vespucci, an Italian explorer and cartographer, played a key role in recognizing the distinct nature of the continents discovered by Columbus. His voyages contributed to the realization that the lands were part of a new continent. The naming of America, derived from his name, reflects his contribution to understanding the geography of the Americas.

Hernán Cortés (1485-1547):
Hernán Cortés, a Spanish conquistador, led the expedition that resulted in the conquest of the Aztec Empire in present-day Mexico. Cortés's success marked a turning point in the colonization of the Americas, bringing immense wealth to Spain and establishing the foundation for further Spanish expansion in the region.

Nicolaus Copernicus (1473-1543):
Nicolaus Copernicus, a Polish mathematician and astronomer, revolutionized the understanding of the cosmos. His heliocentric model, which posited that the Earth and other planets orbited the sun, challenged the geocentric views of the time. Copernicus's work laid the groundwork for the Scientific Revolution and the transformation of astronomy.

Comparative Analysis:
Divergence in Background and Motivations:
Leonardo da Vinci and Christopher Columbus, while contemporaries, diverged significantly in their backgrounds and motivations. Da Vinci, born into the Italian Renaissance, was driven by a thirst for knowledge and a passion for artistic and scientific inquiry. Columbus, on the other hand, emerged from a maritime background in pursuit of a western route to Asia, motivated by economic and geopolitical considerations.

Interdisciplinary Approach vs. Singular Mission:
Leonardo da Vinci's genius lay in his ability to seamlessly integrate art and science, epitomizing the Renaissance ideal of the polymath. His notebooks reveal a holistic approach to

knowledge, where artistic expression and scientific understanding were intertwined. In contrast, Columbus had a singular mission—to find a western route to Asia. While his voyages had profound consequences, they were driven by a specific goal of economic gain and geopolitical advantage.

Global Impact:
Both da Vinci and Columbus left a lasting impact on the world, albeit in different spheres. Da Vinci's influence transcended disciplines, shaping the Renaissance and laying the foundation for future artistic, scientific, and technological advancements. Columbus's impact was felt on a global scale, as his voyages initiated the Age of Discovery, connecting previously isolated parts of the world and reshaping the geopolitical landscape.

Complex Legacies:
The legacies of da Vinci and Columbus are complex and multifaceted. Da Vinci's legacy is celebrated for its contributions to art, science, and innovation. His interdisciplinary approach and the timeless beauty of his artworks continue to inspire generations. Columbus, while celebrated for connecting the Old World and the New World, is also critiqued for the negative consequences of European colonization, including the exploitation and mistreatment of indigenous populations.

Conclusion:
In conclusion, the examination of key figures such as Leonardo da Vinci, Christopher Columbus, and others offers a glimpse into the diverse tapestry of human history. These figures, each

a product of their times, have left an indelible mark on the world through their achievements, endeavors, and the legacies they forged. Leonardo da Vinci's Renaissance brilliance, Christopher Columbus's pioneering voyages, and the contributions of other key figures collectively shaped the trajectory of human civilization, fostering a spirit of exploration, innovation, and intellectual curiosity that continues to resonate through the corridors of time. As we reflect on their lives and impact, we gain insights into the complexity of historical narratives, the interplay of individual genius and societal forces, and the enduring quest for knowledge that propels humanity forward.

Chapter 3: The Industrial Revolution

- **Introduction to the technological advancements and societal changes during the Industrial Revolution**

  Between the late 18th and early 19th century, the world experienced a dramatic transformation in economic, technological, and social conditions known as the Industrial Revolution. During this historic period, output shifted from being dependent on farmers and hand labor to being driven by factories and machines. Modern industrialized civilizations owe a great deal to the interplay between technological progress and sociological shifts that occurred during the Industrial Revolution. In this investigation, we dig into the fundamental technological advances that sparked this revolution and the far-reaching societal changes that followed.

  Innovations in technology:
  The textile sector was the first to embrace mechanization, which played a crucial part in ushering in the Industrial Revolution. The manufacturing of yarn and thread was greatly aided by the development of the spinning jenny, water frame, and spinning mule. These machines greatly improved productivity in the textile industry, cutting down on the need for labor-intensive handiwork and paving the way for later industrialization.

  One of the most revolutionary discoveries of the Industrial Revolution was the steam engine, which generated steam power. James Watt's innovations to the steam engine's design permitted its widespread acceptance throughout industries. Steam engines were used to generate energy for factories, mines, and railroads. This breakthrough signaled a departure from conventional water and wind power in favor of a more flexible and scalable energy source.

The introduction of steam-powered locomotives and ships during the Industrial Revolution radically altered the transportation landscape. The "Rocket" locomotive designed by George Stephenson and first used in 1829 marked the beginning of the age of rail travel. The efficient transport of goods and people thanks to railways became the backbone of industrialized economies. The introduction of steamships also revolutionized sea transport, shortening routes and facilitating more international trade.

Innovations in Metallurgy Advances in metallurgy were critical to the growth of the manufacturing sector. The Bessemer method, developed by Henry Bessemer, allowed for the inexpensive mass manufacture of steel. This breakthrough had extensive effects on the building, manufacturing, and infrastructure industries. Steel allowed architects to create bridges, buildings, and machines that were both larger and more long-lasting.

In the wake of the Industrial Revolution, mass manufacturing of commodities moved away from handiwork and toward mechanization. Many manufacturing operations were mechanized by the introduction of water-powered and then steam-powered technology such as power looms and mechanical saws. This not only boosted productivity but also reduced product prices, making them more affordable for more people.

Improvements in chemistry influenced many sectors, including the textile and farming industries. The introduction of synthetic dyes revolutionized the textile business by expanding color options beyond what could be achieved with natural dyes and decreasing waste. The development of the Haber-Bosch method in the early 20th century also greatly increased agricultural output by modernizing the creation of fertilizer.

Alterations in Society:
The urbanization process began with the vast migration of people from the countryside to cities during the Industrial Revolution. People moved to cities in search of work as new industries and factories cropped up. Industrial cities grew as a result of urbanization, bringing with them overcrowding, pollution, and the emergence of a new urban working class.

The rise of factories and mechanical production brought forth the factory system, which relied on wage labor instead of handcrafted techniques. Men, women, and children alike all found work in factories and endured long shifts and difficult conditions. Many people used to work for free on their families' farms, but that changed with the advent of wage labor.

Social stratification and the emergence of new social classes can be directly attributed to the industrial revolution. The factory owners and capitalists that made up the industrial bourgeoisie surged to power. Meanwhile, the working class, or industrial proletariat, faced difficult circumstances and frequently fought for higher wages and more secure working conditions. As income gaps expanded, social stratification deepened.

The traditional family unit has evolved as a result of the changing nature of work and employment. Family members commonly worked side by side in agricultural communities. However, the factory system contributed to the growing divide between the workplace and the family. The house mostly became a place for family life as adults and children alike found employment in factories. Family structure and social dynamics as a whole were significantly affected by this change.

The result was a dramatic increase in the participation of women and children in the industrial workforce. Factories commonly employed women and children due to their lower wages, smaller hands for complicated work, and the assumption that they were more submissive. This prompted worries about unsafe working conditions and child labor, as well as initiatives to expand protections for low-wage workers.

Trade unions and labor movements emerged in response to the difficult conditions workers faced in workplaces. There was a strike for more pay, reduced hours, and safer working conditions. As the industrial workforce sought to redress the unfairness and sufferings they encountered in a rapidly industrializing society, strikes and protests were commonplace.

Effects on Learning and Understanding
Rise of Public Education: The Industrial Revolution had a major impact on education. The need of having a knowledgeable and educated workforce became more widely acknowledged as industrialization advanced. As a result, several developed countries set up universal public school systems. The objective was to give more people access to elementary school so they could learn the skills necessary for working in factories.

The technological developments of the Industrial Revolution required a workforce with a certain level of technological literacy. Literacy standards grew to encompass more than just reading and writing, but also the use of tools and a comprehension of how factories function. This change in curriculum reflected the requirements of an industrializing society.

Threats and Countermeasures:
Movements for social reform were launched in response to the difficulties and disparities that industrialization spawned. Advocates like Robert Owen and Charles Fourier suggested alternative models of society, emphasizing cooperation, social welfare, and the development of utopian communities. Later struggles for worker rights and social justice were influenced by these concepts.

Taking its name from the legendary character Ned Ludd, the Luddite movement arose in response to the fears that mechanization posed to the handicraft industry. Luddites, who were typically highly skilled artisans, destroyed machinery as a form of protest against mechanization. The movement brought attention to the social disruption brought on by technological progress and the pushback against the eradication of traditional skills.

Labor rules and regulations were established in response to the difficulties workers encountered throughout the industrial period. Governments enacted laws in response to public outcry over issues like unsafe working conditions, the use of child labor, and unfair labor practices. Workers' rights, minimum wage requirements, and prohibitions on child labor are all examples of how labor laws have progressed throughout time.

Conclusion:
As a result of a confluence of scientific progress and socioeconomic shifts, the Industrial Revolution was a defining point in human history. Products were made and economies were organized very differently before and after the introduction of automation, steam power, and mass manufacturing. Urbanization, the advent of industrial capitalism, and the establishment of new social strata were only a few examples of the dramatic societal transformations that accompanied these technological advancements.

Both the material and immaterial conditions of human life were profoundly altered by the Industrial Revolution. It spawned labor movements, social reforms, and legal changes, all of which had never been seen before. Industrialization paved the way for the complex and interconnected global societies we live in today, the effects of which are still being felt in the modern world. When thinking back on the Industrial Revolution, it's important to recognize not only the technological breakthroughs that spurred human progress, but also the social forces that affected people's everyday lives during that turbulent yet revolutionary time.

- **Exploration of key inventions and their impact on manufacturing and transportation**

A radical shift in how cultures treated manufacturing and transportation occurred during the key late 18th/early 19th century period known as the Industrial Revolution. Inventions of this century were crucial in changing the face of many different industries, as well as speeding up manufacturing and altering the transportation scene on a worldwide scale. Important innovations of the Industrial Revolution are investigated, along with their far-reaching effects on industries like manufacturing and transportation.

Industrial Revolution:
The Spinning Jenny, developed by James Hargreaves in the 1760s, revolutionized the textile business. The increased efficiency of textile factories was measured in terms of spin cycles per hour thanks to this multi-spindle spinning frame. Mechanized textile production began with the invention of the Spinning Jenny, which laid the path for further developments in the field.

The Water Frame, invented by Richard Arkwright in the 1760s, was a significant step in automating the textile industry. The yarns spun by this water-powered machine were stronger and finer than those spun by earlier systems. Using water as a source of electricity allowed manufacturers to expand their operations, hastening the departure from home-based industry.

The Power Loom, invented by Edmund Cartwright and patented in 1785, eliminated the need for human labor in the weaving process. The Power Loom, powered by water or steam, allowed for the industrial manufacture of textiles and helped to standardize fabric quality. This development was a major milestone in the mechanization of the textile manufacturing industry as a whole.

Henry Bessemer's invention of the Bessemer Process for mass-producing steel sparked a technological revolution in the middle of the 19th century. A more efficient and inexpensive way of producing steel was developed by blowing air through molten iron to eliminate impurities. The Bessemer Process paved the way for the widespread manufacture of steel, which has since become vital to many sectors, including building and transportation.

James Watt's late-18th-century steam engine was a game-changer that propelled the development of the industrial economy. The steam engine was first developed to pump water from underground mines, but it has since found uses in other types of manufacturing. The Industrial Revolution would not have been possible without its implementation in workplaces and modes of transportation, especially railways and steamships.

Long-distance communication was greatly aided by Samuel Morse's development of Morse code, which was made possible by the advent of the telegraph. The quick transfer of information over enormous distances made possible by the telegraph, which was patented in 1837, revolutionized the way businesses were run. It was crucial in managing logistics, organizing shipping times, and easing cross-border commerce.

Manufacturing Impact:
Productivity Boost: Inventions like the Spinning Jenny and the Power Loom led to a dramatic rise in factory output after mechanization was introduced to the manufacturing process. The increased availability of products and the expansion of consumer markets resulted from factories' ability to produce them on a much greater scale than old artisanal methods.

The widespread use of machinery throughout the manufacturing process led to a generalization of product quality. For instance, the Power Loom would allow for the production of homogeneous and high-quality fabrics. By establishing interchangeable parts and consistent product quality, standardization not only increased production efficiency but also facilitated mass consumption.

Change from Cottage Industry to Factory output New manufacturing technologies brought about a transition from small-scale cottage industries to large-scale factory output. Water and steam powered machinery in factories fueled the industrial revolution. The movement of laborers from farms to cities and industry has far-reaching effects on the structure of the labor force.

Industrialization and economic expansion were made possible by the vast improvements in manufacturing's productivity and scale. Previously labor-intensive and small-scale industries may now scale up to suit the needs of growing consumer markets. Increased manufacturing production helped propel industrial capitalism and give birth to today's leading industrial powers.

While the adoption of factory-based production meant the end of hand-crafted goods, it also ushered in a new era of urbanization and job creation. Many people found work in factories as the economy grew. This inflow of laborers led to urbanization as people traveled from rural areas to cities in pursuit of jobs in the expanding industrial centers.

Transforming the Transportation Industry:
George Stephenson's "Rocket" steam locomotive, introduced in 1829, was the first of its kind and forever changed the face of land travel. Horse-drawn carts were replaced with steam locomotives driven by high-pressure steam engines, drastically improving the efficiency and speed of overland travel. The development of railways facilitated the transport of both people and products.

Steamships were developed when steam power was applied to oceangoing vessels. One of the first commercially viable steamships was Robert Fulton's Clermont, which set sail in 1807. Reduced travel time for long-distance excursions and increased trade volume were both made possible by the advent of steamships.

While not an invention per such, canal building nonetheless contributed greatly to transportation during the Industrial Revolution. The construction of canals facilitated the rapid movement of products between upland regions and coastal harbors. With the opening of the Bridgewater Canal in 1761, England saw a canal-building boom that made it easier to transport both raw materials and finished goods.

The extensive implementation of railway networks radically altered the character of global transportation. Railways enabled for the quick and cost-effective transfer of goods and people over great distances. In order to facilitate the provision of raw materials to manufacturers and the transit of finished goods to markets, railway networks were built to connect key industrial locations.

Expansion of Roads: The upgrading and expansion of road networks were vital to the transportation revolution. John McAdam pioneered a method of constructing roadways by covering them with crushed stone called macadamization. Horse-drawn carriages, carts, and eventually automobiles benefited from the enhanced durability and efficiency of roadways made possible by this development.

Transportation Impact:
Acceleration of Trade: The advances in transportation, particularly steamships and railways, boosted the pace of global trade. It was now possible to rapidly and affordably move raw materials, completed items, and commodities across

great distances. This increased pace of trade helped to link economies around the world.

Because of transportation advancements, the market was able to grow. The market for manufactured goods from urban centers expanded. Because of improvements in long-distance shipping, regional and international trade expanded, bringing diverse regions closer together economically.

The growth of transportation infrastructure, especially railroads, was a major factor in the urbanization and regional development of industrialized countries. Cities grew to become the economic and transportation nerve centers of their regions, while prosperous areas were those with well-developed transportation networks.

Increased mobility made possible by better transit networks fostered interaction between people of different backgrounds and traditions. There would be less restriction on the movement of people, ideas, and cultural norms from one area or country to another. Cultural identities were molded, intellectual movements were sparked, and global variety was enriched as a result of this interaction.

Mobility and Accessibility: Advances in transportation have made travel easier for the general public. The capacity to travel by train or steamship made transportation more accessible to a greater segment of the population. This unprecedented mobility not only changed the face of work and commuting, but also had far-reaching social repercussions, breaking down geographical barriers and bringing people closer together.

Problems and Objections:
The fast industrialization and growth of transportation during this time period had serious effects on the environment. Air pollution was exacerbated by the use of coal to fuel steam engines and manufacturing facilities. Ecosystems in the area may have suffered as a result of human interference during canal and railroad building.

While technological advancements in industry and transportation opened up new avenues for economic growth, they were also linked to the exploitation of workers. Factory workers generally faced long hours, bad working conditions, and low wages. The expansion of cities resulted in overcrowding and poor sanitation for the working class.

Disparities in Society: Not everyone benefited from industrialization and better transportation. Industrialists and factory owners grew rich while workers in many cases struggled to make ends meet. Tension and conflict arose as a result of the widening gap between the industrial bourgeoisie and the industrial proletariat.

Traditional industries were severely impacted by the fast transformations ushered in by technological advances. Mechanized and mass-produced commodities from industrialized factories posed a threat to cottage industries, which relied on manual labor and artisanal craftsmanship. As a result, many long-held cultural and economic practices began to fade.

Conclusion:

In sum, the Industrial Revolution was a watershed era defined by a constellation of game-changing innovations that revolutionized the production and transportation sectors. Humanity was catapulted into a new era of economic, technological, and societal revolution by these inventions, which were driven by the brilliance of innovators and fueled by the persistent spirit of development. Inventions such as the Spinning Jenny, steam engine, power loom, steam locomotive, and telegraph were more than just that; they sparked a global paradigm change.

These innovations have far-reaching and varied effects. They ushered in a period of greater efficiency, product standardization, and the shift away from handcrafted to factory-made goods in the manufacturing sector. The development of the steam engine, trains, steamships, and improved roads greatly impacted the transportation industry, allowing for faster trade, more rapid urbanization, and easier communication between previously isolated areas.

This period of technological advancement, however, was not free of problems and criticism. Significant problems, such as environmental damage, labor exploitation, social inequality, and the effect on established sectors, accompanied the quick transformations. However, the Industrial Revolution set in motion a trajectory of growth that continues to affect our society, economics, and technology environments today. It's important to recognize the era's successes and its challenges as we look back on a time that changed the trajectory of human history forever.

- **Analysis of the social and economic consequences, including urbanization and the rise of capitalism**

  The Industrial Revolution, stretching from the late 18th to the early 19th century, was a watershed point in human history, significantly transforming the socio-economic fabric of societies. The effects of the industrial and transportation revolutions brought about by technical progress were far-reaching and far-reaching. This study examines the complex web of societal and economic changes, zeroing in on the urbanization and capitalist expansion that marked this historical era.

  The Rise of Capitalism and the Shifting Economic Landscape:
  The Industrial Revolution saw a dramatic change in economic systems, one that marked the end of rural economies and the beginning of industrial capitalism. Industrialized economies, driven by machinery, factories, and mass manufacturing of goods, displaced traditional agrarian cultures, which relied on manual labor, small-scale production, and an emphasis on subsistence farming.

  Economic shifts were largely fueled by innovations in technology, such as the steam engine, automated machinery, and the Bessemer process. These developments raised output levels, which in turn made mass manufacture of commodities possible and fueled economic expansion. Industrial capitalism, characterized by its emphasis on capital investment in technology, emerged with the widespread use of machines in manufacturing.

Accumulation of Capital and Entrepreneurship: Industrial capitalism encouraged the accumulation of capital through the investments of business owners and industrialists in things like production facilities and transportation networks. Profit-seeking capitalists had a major impact on the development of the economy. Strong industrial elites with substantial economic clout emerged alongside the growth of industrial capitalism.

Joint-stock firms were established because massive amounts of money had to be invested into various businesses. By forming such organizations, financiers were able to combine their resources and divide up the risks and rewards. Capital was consolidated through the rise of joint-stock firms, which aided economic growth in areas such as mining, railroads, and manufacturing.

The rise of industrial capitalism paved the way for increased market competition and international trade. The surplus of goods made possible by mass production fueled the growth of domestic and global marketplaces. Transportation advancements facilitated a rise in global trade by making it easier to transfer finished products and primary materials around the world.

Urbanization and the Shifting Face of Society:
One of the most obvious social effects of the Industrial Revolution was the movement of large numbers of people

from rural areas to newly developed urban centers. A large percentage of the populace abandoned their agricultural roots in favor of urban centers and factory jobs. Cities expanded rapidly in size and population, and urbanization began to define the age.

Rapid industrialization and factory growth caused the growth of small towns into thriving industrial metropolis. Cities like Pittsburgh and Detroit in the United States and Manchester, Birmingham, and Glasgow in the United Kingdom are great examples of the growth of industrial metropolitan centers. These cities became epicenters of economic activity, innovation, and social transformation.

A new working class emerged as a result of the movement of people from rural areas to urban manufacturing centers. Women and children, as well as adults, worked long hours in dangerous conditions at factories. Factories were often overcrowded and dirty, workers were paid poorly, and their rights were severely restricted. The working class was frequently exploited by business owners looking to increase profits.

Different social classes emerged throughout the Industrial Revolution, with their own set of responsibilities and opportunities. The factory owners, capitalists, and entrepreneurs who made up the industrial bourgeoisie controlled the economy. The working class, or industrial proletariat, on the other hand, endured economic hardships and fought for improved working conditions and worker protections.

The traditional family unit was disrupted by the dramatic shifts that occurred in the nature of work and employment. Family members commonly worked side by side in agricultural communities. Work and domestic responsibilities became more distinct with the advent of factory-based production. The house mostly became a place for family life as adults and children alike found employment in factories.

Difficulties and Community Reactions:
Labor Movements and Trade Unions: The challenges faced by the working class in industrial cities led the establishment of labor movements and trade unions. There was a strike for more pay, reduced hours, and safer working conditions. As the industrial workforce sought to redress the unfairness and sufferings they encountered in a rapidly industrializing society, strikes and protests were commonplace.

Taking its name from the legendary character Ned Ludd, the Luddite movement arose in response to the fears that mechanization posed to the handicraft industry. Luddites, who were typically highly skilled artisans, destroyed machinery as a form of protest against mechanization. The movement brought attention to the social disruption brought on by technological progress and the pushback against the eradication of traditional skills.

Movements for social reform were launched in response to the difficulties and disparities that industrialization spawned. Advocates like Robert Owen and Charles Fourier suggested alternative models of society, emphasizing cooperation, social welfare, and the development of utopian communities. Later struggles for worker rights and social justice were influenced by these concepts.

Consequences for Girls and Little Ones

The Industrial Revolution significantly altered women's participation in the labor force. It wasn't just men and kids that joined the industrial workforce; women did, too. Women were commonly hired by factories because they were paid less than men, had smaller hands, and were more suited to performing complicated tasks.

During the Industrial Revolution, child labor was widely used, prompting moral debate. Many children from low-income families were forced to work in industries. Legislation to limit and control child labor was enacted as a result of social reform movements that focused on ending the abuse of children in the workplace.

Industrialization and the subsequent migration to urban areas had a significant effect on family dynamics. Traditional gender roles have shifted as both men and women have entered the industrial workforce. Previously, men were seen as breadwinners and women as homemakers. The dynamics of families, schools, and daycares were all affected by these shifts.

Learning and Understanding:

As a result of the advancements made during the Industrial Revolution, public schools were able to rise to prominence.

Many industrialized countries' public education systems were established because of the necessity for a trained and literate labor force. The objective was to give more people access to elementary school so they could learn the skills necessary for working in factories.

The technological developments of the Industrial Revolution required a workforce with a certain level of technological literacy. Literacy standards grew to encompass more than just reading and writing, but also the use of tools and a comprehension of how factories function. This change in curriculum reflected the requirements of an industrializing society.

Impacts on Culture and Morality:
The rapid pace of industrialization and urbanization has given rise to a number of difficult moral questions. Concerns were voiced over the unethical treatment of workers, the destruction of the environment, and the disparity in wealth. Concerns about the ethical obligations of industrialists, the fair treatment of employees, and the repercussions of unchecked capitalism on society were raised.

The cultural landscape shifted drastically throughout the Industrial Revolution. A more industrial and economic mentality replaced the old ways of thinking, which had their roots in rural life and handiwork. New forms of artistic, literary, and intellectual expression emerged as cities drew people from different backgrounds together.

Threats and Countermeasures:
Labor rules and regulations were established in response to the difficulties workers encountered throughout the industrial period. Governments enacted laws in response to public outcry over issues like unsafe working conditions, the use of child labor, and unfair labor practices. Workers' rights, minimum wage requirements, and prohibitions on child labor are all examples of how labor laws have progressed throughout time.

Responses to the social and economic pressures brought on by industrialization gave rise to social reform movements. Robert Owen, who proposed the concept of cooperative communities, and the trade union movement attempted to alleviate the economic disparities and better the lives of the working class. Later attempts for worker rights and social justice built on the foundations established by these movements.

Philosophical Reactions: Many different schools of thought emerged in response to the Industrial Revolution's impact on society and the economy. For instance, Karl Marx criticized capitalism and predicted a proletarian uprising. Meanwhile, Adam Smith and other proponents of laissez-faire capitalism argued that open markets and individual initiative were superior to government regulation.

Conclusion:
As a result of its scientific advancements, economic alterations, and social effects, the Industrial Revolution ultimately altered

the course of human history. The advent of industrial capitalism, typified by capital accumulation, entrepreneurship, and market expansion, created the groundwork for current economic systems. Urbanization, the creation of separate social classes, and the struggles of the working class all occurred simultaneously.

Progress and exploitation coexisted during the Industrial Revolution, making it a time of great paradoxes. Significant social obstacles, ethical dilemmas, and arguments about the role of government and industry in addressing societal ills accompanied the benefits of economic expansion and technical advancement. When thinking back on this revolutionary era, it's important to recognize its layered complexity, including the technological advances that propelled human progress and the social, economic, and ethical factors that shaped people's everyday lives.

- **Examination of the role of industrialization in shaping the modern world**

  The Industrial Revolution was a watershed moment in human history due to the magnitude of the technological and economic changes it brought about. The era of industrialization, which began in the late 18th and continued into the early 19th century, was one of the most transformative in human history. This study looks at how industrialization has affected the world in many different ways, including the economy, culture, and geography.

  Globalization, Industrialization, and Economic Change:
  Shift from Agrarian to Industrial Economies: Industrialization signaled a major shift from agrarian-based economies to industrial economies. Traditional communities that relied on manual labor and rural methods gave way to a new era in which machinery, factories, and mass production became the primary engines of economic activity. The economic structures we know and use today can trace their roots to this era of transformation.

  The rise of Industrial Capitalism Industrialization marked the beginning of the transition from handicrafts to mass manufacturing in factories. Industrialists, businesspeople, and investors amassed vast amounts of wealth as the economy expanded thanks to their inventions, technologies, and business acumen. The capitalist systems that support today's economies have their genesis in this change.

The growth of capital and the spirit of enterprise were defining features of the industrial revolution. Machines, factories, and infrastructure were built by businesspeople and industrialists who hoped to boost output and cut costs. This capital-driven strategy not only disrupted entire industries, but it also propelled the growth of international trade and facilitated the integration of economies around the world.

Changes in Society:
One of the most noticeable results of industrialization was the explosive expansion of major cities. The transformation of rural areas into thriving manufacturing hubs prompted a large exodus of people looking for work. Industrial cities like Manchester, Birmingham, and Pittsburgh emerged as economic powerhouses, and their urbanization became a defining feature of the contemporary world.

Different social classes emerged as a result of the industrial revolution, with their own responsibilities and opportunities. The factory owners and capitalists made up the industrial bourgeoisie, who controlled economic power, while the working class, known as the industrial proletariat, struggled with difficult working conditions. This separation into social classes became a hallmark of contemporary civilizations.

The traditional family unit was impacted by the dramatic shifts that occurred in the nature of work and employment. Family members commonly worked side by side in agricultural communities. Work and domestic responsibilities became more distinct with the advent of factory-based production. The house mostly became a place for family life as adults and children alike found employment in factories.

Impact of New Technologies Around the World:
Innovations in technology were the driving force behind the industrial revolution. The Bessemer process, the power loom, the spinning jenny, and other inventions similarly altered the manufacturing landscape. These developments not only boosted efficiency and output, but also set the path for other breakthroughs in the contemporary age.

The effects of industrialization were felt across boundaries and helped to further the development of international relationships. Transportation advancements like steamships and railroads made it easier to carry goods and people across oceans. Globalization of economies and the subsequent increase in trade between countries are two of the distinguishing features of the modern world.

Large-scale changes to the cultural landscape occurred during the industrial revolution. A more industrial and economic mentality replaced the old ways of thinking, which had their roots in rural life and handiwork. Cities became crossroads for people of all backgrounds to interact and learn from one another, creating a rich tapestry of modern global culture.

Intellectual Reactions to Industrialization People had different reactions to the social changes brought on by industrialization. Karl Marx and other scholars criticized capitalism and predicted a proletarian uprising. The free market and the initiative of individuals were also defended by those like Adam

Smith. The economic and political beliefs of the modern world can be traced back to these philosophical discussions.

Threats and Countermeasures:
Trade unions and labor movements emerged in response to the difficulties experienced by the working class in urban centers that housed major manufacturing facilities. There was a strike for more pay, reduced hours, and safer working conditions. These uprisings sprang from the struggles of the working class in an increasingly industrialized society.

Luddite Movement: The Luddite movement, developed out of the perceived risks of automation to traditional handicraft, emerged as a response to industrialization. Luddites, who were typically highly skilled artisans, destroyed machinery as a form of protest against mechanization. The upheaval in society brought on by technological advances was highlighted, as was the pushback against the eradication of traditional skills.

Effects on the Environment:
Environmental Degradation: The rapid industrialization and development of companies have substantial environmental implications. Air pollution was exacerbated by the use of coal to fuel steam engines and manufacturing facilities. Ecosystems in the area may have suffered as a result of human interference during canal and railroad building. As a result of its detrimental effects on the environment, industrialization sparked moral debates regarding resource conservation and management.

Although industrialization exacerbated environmental problems, it also sparked a number of inventive technological answers. Cleaner and more efficient manufacturing technologies were developed as part of these process innovations. The dynamic interplay between industrialization and ecological viability has emerged as an essential factor in constructing the contemporary world.

Historical Significance and the Present Day:
Modern society may trace its roots back to the industrial revolution. The economic institutions, technological advances, and social transformations that were initiated during this time period remain influential in today's civilizations. What we have now in terms of technological advancement, globalization of economies, and capitalism systems can be traced back to the Industrial Revolution.

The results of the Industrial Revolution are still having an impact on modern society, providing both difficulties and possibilities. Even while income inequality, environmental degradation, and labor exploitation still exist, living conditions and connectivity have increased thanks to technological improvements. The pursuit of sustainable development and moral corporate practices reflects an ongoing discussion of industrialization's aftereffects.

Conclusion:
In sum, industrialization has played a fundamental and complex role in creating today's world. The Industrial Revolution set in motion economic and societal changes as

well as technological advancements that paved the way for the complex, interconnected, and ever-changing global landscape in which we now find ourselves. The effects of industrialization may be heard throughout history, from the emergence of industrial capitalism to the struggles of the working class, from the worldwide impact of interconnected economies to the continuous discourse on environmental sustainability.

It's important, as we deal with the complexities of today's world, to remember the lessons we picked up during the industrial revolution. There is a rich tapestry of human history because of technological progress, global economic interdependence, and cultural and intellectual responses to societal changes. Understanding the ongoing development of communities, economies, and cultures requires an appreciation of the forces that have shaped the contours of our modern existence, and this can be achieved by focusing on the role of industrialization.

Chapter 4: World Wars I and II

○ Overview of the causes and consequences of World War I

The First World War, or the Great War, began in 1914 and lasted until 1918 on every continent. Major international powers were involved in this tragic war, which caused unimaginable devastation and loss of life. The political, economic, military, and diplomatic factors that led to World War I are intertwined and interdependent. The war had far-reaching repercussions, altering the geopolitical landscape, transforming societies, and setting the stage for future wars. This summary will go into the complex network of events and effects that shaped one of the most pivotal periods in human history.

Factors that led to WWI
The rise of nationalism was crucial in setting the stage for World War I. Rivalry and competition erupted across Europe due to strong senses of national pride and devotion. The Balkans, in particular, witnessed a boom in nationalist sentiments, contributing to tensions in the region. Passion for one's country tends to inflame tensions between nations and increase the chance of war.

The imperialistic era, characterized by competition for colonies and world power, heightened global tensions. Competition for overseas territories arose as European countries strove to expand their empires. The struggle for global hegemony ratcheted up international tensions, tipping an already precarious power balance into chaos.

World War I was fueled, in large part, by the ideology of militarism, which is characterized by the accumulation of military forces and the conviction that military solutions are effective. The major European powers expanded their military forces and technological prowess. The environment was ripe for conflict because of the widespread acceptance of military might as a deterrent and a method of protecting national interests.

The geopolitical landscape became even more complex when alliance systems evolved in the late 19th and early 20th centuries. France, Russia, and the United Kingdom formed the Triple Entente to counteract Germany, Austria-Hungary, and Italy's Triple Alliance. The security and deterrence these alliances were supposed to give was instead replaced with a web of responsibilities that drew more countries into the conflict when it broke out.

The assassination of Archduke Franz Ferdinand of Austria-Hungary on June 28, 1914, at Sarajevo, was the immediate cause of the commencement of World War One. The assassination, carried out by a nationalist Bosnian Serb, triggered a series of dramatic developments. The alliance commitments of other countries, together with Austria-Hungary's declaration of war against Serbia, quickly escalated the conflict.

Failure of Diplomacy: Diplomatic efforts to avert conflict proved fruitless as tensions increased. It was difficult to find diplomatic solutions to the crises that arose because of the complicated system of alliances and the extreme nationalism and militarism of the time. Diplomats toiled in vain to ease tensions, and the breakdown of peaceful communication set the stage for the start of fighting.

The fallout from the First World War:
A stunning number of lives were lost, and many people suffered, during World War I. Trench fighting became commonplace on the Western Front as the conflict progressed. Estimates of casualties range from 15 to 20 million people; these include both combatants and civilians. A whole generation was emotionally and physically damaged by the conflict.

The formal end of World War I and the imposition of large territorial changes on the vanquished Central Powers were both enshrined in the Treaty of Versailles, which was signed in 1919. As the Austro-Hungarian and Ottoman Empires collapsed, new states formed on their former territory. The redrawing of Germany's borders caused seismic alterations in European geopolitics as a result of the country's massive reparations and territory losses.

The League of Nations was formed in response to the need for international cooperation to ensure everyone's safety and forestall further wars. The purpose of the League was to serve as a platform for the discussion, negotiation, and implementation of international solutions. But the League's efforts were in vain, and the Second World War nevertheless broke out.

The Great War's economy-wide effects were significant. National economies were stressed by the war effort, which resulted in high levels of debt and financial instability. Germany's economy suffered as a result of the reparations required by the Treaty of Versailles, setting the groundwork for the difficulties of the interwar period.

Alterations to the Political System: The end of World War I brought about profound changes to the political system in Europe. New political entities rose to power as monarchies collapsed. The Russian Revolution of 1917 culminated in the founding of a socialist state, while the collapse of empires led to the creation of new states in Central and Eastern Europe. The conflict was a major factor in the development of 20th-century political ideology.

Authoritarian and totalitarian regimes gained power as a result of the instability produced by World War I. The rise of Adolf Hitler and the Nazi Party in Germany may be traced back to the country's economic woes and growing unrest. In a similar vein, the war's aftermath paved the way for the establishment of authoritarian regimes across Europe, including Italy.

The effects of World War I on culture and the development of ideas were far-reaching. Artistic and literary movements of the 1920s, such as Dada and existentialism, expressed the disillusionment and trauma suffered by war combatants. As a result of the war's violence and pointless devastation, conventional wisdom was challenged.

The unresolved difficulties and grievances from World War I served as a catalyst for the escalation of tensions that led to World War II. Unresolved geopolitical conflicts, economic uncertainty, and the harsh provisions of the Treaty of Versailles all contributed to the rise of aggressive regimes and the resumption of global strife.

unanswered matters as a Cause of Ongoing Geopolitical Tensions The peace treaty that ended World War I left many matters unanswered. The punitive tone of the Treaty of Versailles and the inability to address the underlying causes of the war both contributed to the emergence of new conflicts and increased regional instability.

Importance in History and Important Lessons
Diplomatic Lesson: The First World War I teaches us the value of talking things out and finding peaceful solutions to conflicts. Diplomatic efforts to avert the war proved futile, highlighting the necessity for effective international institutions and methods to resolve crises without resorting to military force.

A Word of Caution Regarding Harsh Reparations: It is widely believed that the economic problems and political instability that preceded World War II were exacerbated by the severe reparations placed on Germany by the Treaty of Versailles. The lesson is that long-term peace and security can only be achieved through equitable and enduring post-conflict settlements.

The League of Nations was formed in part because of the need for international collaboration and collective security. Despite the League's failure, it inspired other attempts to establish international organizations with the goal of averting conflict and set a precedent for such efforts.

World War I had a significant effect on military strategy and the way wars were fought. Tanks and chemical weapons are just two examples of how the advent of new technology altered the character of war. The war's lessons molded military strategy during World War II and informed decisions during the interwar period.

Conclusion:
In sum, World War I was a watershed moment that determined the whole 20th century. The complicated web of reasons, from nationalism and militarism to intricate alliance networks, resulted to a conflict of unprecedented scope and suffering. Immediate and long-term effects of the conflict were far-reaching, affecting everything from the geopolitical landscape and political systems to the way people thought and felt about the world.

The lessons to be learned from World War I include the perils of ineffective diplomacy, the dangers of punitive reparations, and the necessity of getting at the roots of conflict in order to forestall its recurrence. Lessons learned from the war's aftermath continue to inform contemporary debates about diplomacy, international relations, and the search for global peace and stability. Thinking about what led up to and followed from World violence I helps shed light on the nuances of interpersonal relationships, the weight of geopolitical choices, and the never-ending search for a world without violence.

- **Examination of the interwar period and the lead-up to World War II**

  World War I ended in 1918, and the years between then and the start of World War II in 1939 were known as the "interwar period," a time of great upheaval and complexity. This time period, marked by political and economic upheaval and the search for new international orders, paved the way for the later global battle. This analysis dives into the complexities of the years between the wars, looking at the causes of the instability of peace, the growth of authoritarian governments, and the mounting geopolitical tensions that led to the start of World War II.

  First World War's Lasting Effects:
  Europe and the rest of the globe had to deal with the fallout of the terrible First globe War. Germany was punished severely by losing territory, having its military severely restricted, and paying large reparations under the terms of the Treaty of Versailles, which was signed in 1919. Resentment and economic sufferings caused by the treaty's harsh conditions paved the way for political and social unrest in Germany. New geopolitical difficulties arose as a result of the collapse of empires and the redefinition of borders in Central and Eastern Europe.

  Second, the Great Depression was caused by economic difficulties.
  The Great Depression, which began in 1929, was the most notable economic event of the interwar period. Many

European countries' economies were depleted during the war, and the worldwide economic downturn made matters worse. Joblessness skyrocketed, production in the industrial sector dropped precipitously, and trade deficits widened noticeably. The economic downturn paved the way for the growth of extremist ideologies and political extremism.

Totalitarian regimes' meteoric rise:
Many European countries saw the rise of totalitarian regimes during the years between the wars. The Fascist Party of Benito Mussolini came to power in Italy in 1922; in Germany, Adolf Hitler's National Socialist German Workers' Party (Nazi Party) took over in 1933. These governments glorified the state, stifled dissent, and promoted authoritarian rule. Fascism and Nazism were political movements that aimed to solve social problems, boost national pride, and create authoritative, centralized regimes.

Aggressive foreign policies and territorial expansion by several governments emerged during the interwar period. In 1935, Italy invaded Ethiopia in an attempt to establish a colonial foothold in Africa. Meanwhile, the remilitarization of the Rhineland in 1936 and Germany's annexation of Austria in 1938 (Anschluss) revealed the country's expansionist ambitions. The international response was muted, despite the fact that these measures directly violated the Treaty of Versailles.

5. The League of Nations' Weaknesses
The League of Nations, formed in the wake of World War I to foster international security and forestall further wars, was

helpless in the face of growing aggressiveness. The League's shortcomings were underscored by the fact that it did nothing to stop fascist assault. Its authority was further undermined by the League's inability to stop the Italian invasion of Ethiopia and to take a firm stance against German rearmament.

6. Policies of Appeasement:
Western powers, led by Britain and France, embraced the strategy of appeasement in an effort to defuse tensions by negotiating with aggressors. The Munich Agreement of 1938, which permitted Germany to acquire the Sudetenland from Czechoslovakia, is an example of this technique to dealing with Hitler's early territorial expansion. Although appeasement was supposed to defuse tense situations, it actually served to empower aggressors and make war more likely.

Spanish Civil War, 1936-1939 7.
Conflicts on a global scale had its roots in the Spanish Civil War, which raged from 1936 to 1939 between Republican and Nationalist forces in Spain. Fascist powers such as Germany and Italy intervened in the conflict on the side of General Francisco Franco's Nationalist forces. New military strategies and technology were developed and tested throughout the battle before being implemented on a greater scale during World War II.

In 1939, ideological enemies Nazi Germany and the Soviet Union signed the Molotov-Ribbentrop Pact. The deal comprised a non-aggression pact as well as secret protocols that set up zones of influence over Eastern Europe. This gave Hitler the confidence he needed to launch his invasion of

Poland without worrying about the Soviet Union interfering. While the pact did buy Germany some time, it paved the way for a larger confrontation down the road.

Czechoslovakia's annexation, number nine:
Even after Hitler's demands for the Sudetenland were satisfied by the Munich Agreement, Germany continued its aggressive policies. Germany occupied the rest of Czechoslovakia in March 1939, which was a direct violation of the Munich Agreement. This overt act of aggression highlighted the ineffectiveness of appeasement and increased worries about the growing risk of war in Europe.

World War II Begins with the Nazi Invasion of Poland 10
Germany's invasion of Poland on September 1, 1939, was the final spark that set off global conflict. The Polish fortifications were quickly overcome by Germany's Blitzkrieg tactics, and the Soviet Union invaded from the east in accordance with the secret procedures of the Molotov-Ribbentrop Pact. In response to Germany's invasion of Poland, Britain and France declared war on Germany on September 3, 1939.

Implications of the Cold War Era:
Massive Human Cost: The interwar period set the ground for the most catastrophic battle in human history. Over sixty million people were killed in World War II, an amount that has never been seen before in human history. The genocide, bombings, and extensive destruction that occurred throughout the conflict will forever be etched into the human psyche.

World War II caused a dramatic shift in the international balance of power. The conflict resulted in the rise of the United States and the Soviet Union as global superpowers and the fall of European colonial empires. There was a shift in the international system that set the stage for the Cold War.

During World War II, Nazi Germany committed the systematic genocide known as the Holocaust. Six million Jews were killed in the Holocaust, along with millions of additional victims, including as Romani people, persons with disabilities, and political dissidents. The purpose of the postwar Nuremberg Trials was to prosecute Nazi war criminals.

The United Nations was founded after World War II as an attempt to create a new system for international cooperation and conflict resolution. To further the goals of peace, security, and international collaboration, the League of Nations was succeeded in 1945 by the United Nations (UN). The United Nations was a symbol of a renewed dedication to the use of diplomacy to avoid conflict in the future.

After WWII's destruction in Europe and Asia, massive reconstruction and economic recovery activities were necessary. The United States' Marshall Plan helped rebuild Europe after World War II by providing economic aid to countries in need. There was a period of economic growth and the formation of new political and economic coalitions in the years following World War Two.

Conclusion:

The interwar period, filled with economic hardships, political upheavals, and the emergence of totalitarian governments, lay the framework for the devastating events of World War II. The legacy of this time period is a harsh warning about the perils of unbridled aggression and the failure of diplomacy and appeasement. The peace that had emerged after World War I was too weak to weather the storm of geopolitical tensions and power conflicts that erupted during the decade between the wars.

In retrospect, the years between the world wars stand out as a watershed moment that determined the fate of nations and the 20th century's trajectory. The interwar period taught us that preventing future terrible global conflicts requires attention to their origins, the strengthening of international collaboration, and the promotion of diplomacy. The years between the world wars serve as a warning, imploring the next generation to be ever-vigilant in its pursuit of peace and to draw lessons from the tragic events of World War II.

- **In-depth analysis of key events, battles, and strategies during both wars**

Both World Wars, WWI (1914–1918) and WWII (1939–1945), were catastrophic wars that permanently altered the 20th century's geopolitical landscape and cultural fabric. The critical moments, turning battles, and strategic factors that shaped both wars will be examined in detail. The outcomes of these wars were decided by a complex interaction of military, political, and diplomatic forces, and this was true everywhere from the Western Front trenches to the island-hopping battles of the Pacific.

The assassination of Archduke Franz Ferdinand of Austria-Hungary on June 28, 1914, in Sarajevo, Bosnia, was the precipitating event that led to the commencement of World War One. With its declaration of war against Serbia, Austria-Hungary set off a chain reaction that drew in other major powers through alliances.

There was a lot of trench warfare on the Western Front, when entrenched troops fought a stalemate for long stretches of time. Massive deaths and few territory gains were the consequence of battles like the 1916 Somme and Verdun campaigns, illustrating the difficulties posed by modern weaponry and strong positions.

In 1917, the combat between German and Austro-Hungarian forces and Russian forces became more fluid on the Eastern Front, which also saw a revolution in Russia. War fatigue played a role in the 1917 Russian Revolution that toppled the

Tsar and brought power to the Bolsheviks under Vladimir Lenin.

The year 1917 marked a watershed moment in history as the United States entered World War I. The influx of American troops bolstered the Allies, both in terms of personnel and material supplies. The pivotal battle of Belleau Wood (1918) demonstrated the superiority of American troops in combat.

The Treaty of Versailles and the Closing of the Front (1918–1919):
A string of offensives culminated in the Armistice on November 11, 1918, as the Central Powers collapsed under the weight of their own weariness and the introduction of new Allied forces. The Treaty of Versailles, signed in 1919, included severe punishments for Germany in an effort to forestall further wars. The treaty's harsh terms, however, fueled animosity and set the stage for further conflict.

During WWII:
The German invasion of Poland in September 1939 marked the official start of World War II. Germany was able to quickly overcome Polish defenses by employing Blitzkrieg tactics. While both sides were preparing for larger battles, a period known as the Phony War ensued on the Western Front.

The German Blitzkrieg resumed with the invasion of France in 1940, which led to the country's eventual collapse. German forces' unexpectedly swift march through the Ardennes forest led to the encirclement and eventual defeat of French and

British forces at Dunkirk. The Germans took over Western Europe when France fell, marking a pivotal moment.

The Battle of Britain, fought between 1940 and 1941, was a critical battle for control of British airspace. The RAF successfully defended Britain from German air strikes, stopping an invasion. The British people's fortitude during the Blitz exemplified the value of sophisticated anti-aircraft systems.

The German invasion of the Soviet Union in 1941, known as Operation Barbarossa, was a massive military assault that ultimately changed the course of World War II. The Soviet Union's tenacious defense and the brutal winter weather ultimately did in the Germans. The Soviet Union's victorious counteroffensive in the Battle of Stalingrad (1942–1943) marked a turning point in the war.

The Pacific Theater saw several major naval battles and island-hopping assaults in 1941, including the attack on Pearl Harbor. The United States entered the war after the Japanese attack on Pearl Harbor on December 7, 1941. The Battle of Midway (1942) was a watery showdown that effectively halted Japanese progress throughout the Pacific.

The Allies fought the Axis powers in North Africa during the years of 1942 and 1943 during the North African Campaign and Operation Torch. The campaign was headed by General Bernard Montgomery and then by General Dwight D. Eisenhower. The beginning of the end for Axis forces in Africa may be traced back to 1942, when the Allied invasion of North Africa, codenamed Operation Torch, was a resounding success.

During 1943–1945, the Allies landed in Sicily and pushed across Italy in what is known as the Italian Campaign. Both the terrain and the Axis opposition were difficult to navigate during the campaign. It was a major triumph when Rome fell in 1944, but the battle didn't end until the Germans surrendered in Italy the following year, in 1945.

The Western Front and D-Day (1944-1945)
On June 6, 1944 (D-Day), the Allies launched Operation Overlord, an enormous operation that signaled the beginning of the end for Nazi Germany in Western Europe. Allies were able to push farther into Germany after a successful landing and subsequent liberation of Paris.

The Battle of the Bulge, which lasted from December 1944 to January 1945, was the final major German attack on the Western Front. The surprise onslaught sought to split Allied forces and reach the Belgian port of Antwerp. The Allies were able to regroup and successfully fend off the German attack despite their early advantages.

The War Ends with One Last Effort (1945)
In May of 1945, as Allied forces from the east and west closed in on Germany, the Soviet Union took Berlin. On May 7, 1945, Germany surrendered unconditionally after Hitler committed suicide. The Axis powers were ultimately defeated, and the European war ended.

Pacific Island-Hopping missions (1943-1945): In the Pacific, Allied forces fought in a series of island-hopping missions to seize vital islands from Japanese control. The battles of Guadalcanal, Iwo Jima, and Okinawa were crucial conflicts that moved Allied forces closer to Japan.

The climax of the Pacific War was the August 1945 dropping of atomic bombs on the cities of Hiroshima and Nagasaki. These bombings had such an effect on Japan that on August 15, 1945, the country surrendered, effectively ending World War II.

Strategic and Tactical Focus:
During World War One, the Western Front was characterized by trench warfare. A static and lethal battlefield was the result of massive trench systems, barbed wire, and defended positions. Artillery barrages, chemical attacks, and infantry charges were all used by both sides in an effort to break the deadlock.

The Germans used a military strategy known as blitzkrieg, or "lightning war," during World War II. Blitzkrieg was an offensive strategy that attempted to surprise and disorganize the opposition by rapidly deploying infantry, tanks, and air support. In the beginning of the war, the strategies worked exceptionally well.

Both World Wars witnessed widespread usage of strategic bombing campaigns, which were used extensively throughout World War I and World War II. Air attacks during World War I frequently hit civilian areas as well as hostile installations. The bombing campaign by the Allies against German cities and the strikes by the Axis forces on London and other towns changed the face of warfare forever during World War II.

Both wars relied heavily on naval force, particularly naval warfare and submarine warfare. The deployment of submarines, particularly German U-boats in World War I and the Battle of the Atlantic in World War II, highlighted the importance of sea control. During World Wars I and II, key naval encounters were the Battle of Jutland and the Battle of Midway.

The need to win air battles and establish dominance was a driving factor in both conflicts. Large-scale aerial combat became common during World War II, whereas dogfights amongst fighter planes emerged during World War I. The development of more modern aircraft and air tactics altered the outcome of numerous encounters.

During World War II, amphibious assaults and island-hopping campaigns were used extensively in the Pacific Theater. In order to be successful, missions requiring air, land, and sea forces had to be meticulously planned and coordinated.

Analyzing the Differences:
When comparing World War II to World War I in terms of technology, the latter clearly had the upper hand. New technology, such as long-range missiles and jet engines, and the widespread deployment of these weapons shifted the

character of combat. Critical contributions were also made by advances in radar and code-breaking technologies.

Alliances and globalization: While World War I was primarily fought on European soil, its effects were felt all over the world. Although alliances were complicated in both conflicts, they were much more so during World War II. The United States, the Soviet Union, and the United Kingdom were part of the Allied powers that faced off against the Axis powers, who were commanded by Germany, Japan, and Italy.

The struggle against totalitarian regimes, fascism, and the racial practices of Nazi Germany provided more obvious ideological dimensions to World War II. The conflict highlighted the significance of collective security and international cooperation and had far-reaching consequences for human rights and the postwar formation of the United Nations.

The concept of total war, in which entire societies are mobilized for the war effort, and its effects on civilians were at play in both conflicts. Cities were destroyed, businesses were disrupted, and populations were mobilized for war production, all of which had devastating effects on civilians. The Holocaust and other horrors committed during World War II elevated the concept of total war to new heights.

Conclusion:
Understanding the intricacies and dynamics that shaped World Wars I and II requires an examination of the major events,

battles, and strategies that took place throughout both wars. The conflicts were marked by a confluence of scientific advancement, strategic planning, and the enormous human cost of global battle, from the Western Front trenches to the island-hopping campaigns of the Pacific.

The immobility of trench warfare and the geopolitical repercussions of the Treaty of Versailles defined World War I and set the stage for subsequent wars. The Blitzkrieg tactics, strategic bombing campaigns, and ideological components of World War II rearranged the global power structure and paved the way for the Cold War.

The lessons learnt from these battles continue to affect military thinking, diplomatic ties, and international cooperation. Looking back on the hardships and struggles of these eras, it's clear that studying these pivotal events and techniques isn't just an academic exercise; it's also essential for making sense of the intricacies of global conflict and creating a more peaceful tomorrow.

- **Discussion of the profound social, political, and economic changes resulting from the wars**

  Changes in the social, political, and economic structures of countries all over the world were precipitated by the end of World Wars I and II. These wars, separated by only two decades, permanently altered the course of human events, with repercussions felt for many years to come. The enormous effects of the wars are explored here through an analysis of the complex relationship between social, political, and economic forces that created the world after the wars.

  Changes in Society:
  Human Cost and Trauma: The wars exacted a tremendous human toll, with millions of lives lost and countless others forever transformed. Scars were left on national psyches from the agony endured by soldiers and civilians alike. In the form of post-traumatic stress disorder (PTSD), the lifelong psychological toll of war was brought home.

  During both wars, established gender roles began to change. Women were able to enter the workforce in record numbers as men were called to the front lines. Women's efforts during the wars pushed the boundaries of gender roles and laid the framework for the emergence of women's liberation movements in the decades that followed.

  Major population shifts occurred as a result of the wars, particularly World War I's loss of a generation of young men and World War II's baby boom. As people were uprooted and forced to find new homes and livelihoods, migration patterns emerged as a direct result of the reorganization of society.

Wars had a significant impact on the cultural landscape, which included expression and artistic movements. Artistic forms like dada and surrealism emerged during the interwar period to process the trauma and disillusionment of World War I. The horrors and ideological battles of World War II sparked existentialism and new approaches to narrative in the visual and performing arts.

Awareness of human rights issues was catalyzed by the disclosure of the Holocaust and the systematic slaughter committed by the Nazis during World War II. After World War II, the Nuremberg Trials established a legal standard for trying war criminals, criminals against humanity, and perpetrators of genocide.

Changes in Politics
Dismantling of Empires and Redrawing of Borders The treaties that ended both wars also resulted in the redrawing of borders and decolonization. After World War I, the Austro-Hungarian and Ottoman Empires collapsed, and European colonial empires were threatened. Decolonization campaigns gained impetus in the post-World War II era, resulting to the independence of numerous states.

In 1945, in reaction to the League of Nations' failure and the lessons learnt from the wars, the United Nations (UN) was founded. The United Nations was established as a platform for diplomatic negotiations and conflict resolution with the goal of fostering international collaboration, peace, and security. The United Nations was established because of a desire to forestall further international hostilities.

Conflict between the United States and its Western allies and the Soviet Union and the Eastern Bloc was a geopolitical battle that cemented the ideological divides that had arisen during the wars. The ideological standoff between communism and capitalism defined the bipolar world order that dominated international affairs for a large portion of the postwar era.

During the Cold War, two major military alliances emerged: the North Atlantic Treaty Organization (NATO) and the Warsaw Pact. The Western democracies that made up NATO wanted to stop the spread of communism, while the Soviet Union-led Warsaw Pact hoped to keep communist republics in Eastern Europe in power.

Democracy's precariousness was highlighted by the rise of totalitarian regimes in the interwar period and during World War II, and authoritarian ideas were shown to have widespread appeal. After World War II, discussions on government, human rights, and the role of the state were shaped by fascism and Nazism's influence.

Changing Economic Conditions:
Wars wreaked havoc on economies all around the world, necessitating extensive rebuilding efforts afterward. Initiated

by the United States, the Marshall Plan gave economic aid to war-torn European nations, assisting in their road to recovery and stability in the years following World War II. The EEC and, later, the EU were built on the economic foundations established during the restoration operations.

The Military-Industrial Complex and Rapid Technological Developments

Aviation, medicine, and communication all benefited from the boost in innovation that the wars provided. The wartime emergence of the military-industrial complex persisted into the immediate postwar years. Innovation and economic growth were both sparked by the transformation of wartime industry into peacetime producers.

The economic superpowers that arose in the wake of World War II—the United States and the Soviet Union, in particular—emerged as global hegemons. After World War II, nations began to engage in international trade and collaboration as a means of economic recovery and growth.

The economic boom and emergence of consumer culture that followed World War II are often considered to go hand in hand. The economic boom in the United States, known as the "Golden Age of Capitalism," fuelled a spike in consumer spending, suburbanization, and technical innovation. The ripple effects of this economic growth were seen in all aspects of society and daily life.

The International Monetary Fund (IMF) and the World Bank were created following the 1944 Bretton Woods Conference in an effort to promote international monetary stability and stimulate international trade. These organizations were instrumental in establishing a secure worldwide monetary system and reorganizing the global economy after World War Two.

Difficulties and Footprints:
Nuclear proliferation and the ensuing arms race were major threats to international safety after the Second World War saw the advent of nuclear weapons. A nuclear holocaust became a more real possibility as a result of the Cold War armaments race between the United States and the Soviet Union. Strategic planning and international talks were affected by the idea of mutually assured destruction (MAD).

The damage of landscapes during warfare and the long-term repercussions of military technologies both had significant negative effects on the environment. The environmental costs of war were made obvious by the employment of chemical weapons in World War I and the testing of nuclear weapons in the postwar period.

Humanitarian issues: The battles left a legacy of humanitarian issues, notably the fate of refugees and displaced persons. International humanitarian law and organizations arose as a result of efforts to meet the needs of survivors, especially those who had witnessed or been a victim of atrocities.

The wars sparked a collective resolve to learn from their mistakes and forestall future world hostilities. A determination to avoid repeating previous errors can be seen in the creation of international institutions, the advancement of human rights, and diplomatic efforts aimed at conflict resolution.

Conclusion:
The world was forever altered by the political, social, and economic shifts that followed World Wars I and II. The wounds of conflict, both apparent and invisible, altered the course of nations and individuals. There was a fine line between peace and security after World War II and the drive for advancement and the fear of another violence.

Recognizing the resiliency of human communities in the face of tragedy is essential when we consider the profound impact of the wars. The wars have taught us the value of working together across borders, using diplomatic channels, and having a firm dedication to defending values like peace, justice, and human rights. The lessons of the post-war era can help us comprehend the difficulties of the present and chart a course for the future that emphasizes mutual respect and the goal of world peace.

Chapter 5: The Digital Revolution and the Information Age

- **Examination of the role of industrialization in shaping the modern world**

    The advent of digital technology in the late 20th century and its continued development into the 21st century have brought about a dramatic change in the manner in which people, organizations, and communities disseminate and discuss information. The development of digital technology has not only increased the efficiency and convenience of communication, but it has also changed the fundamental nature of how we share and receive information. This essay delves into the historical origins, technological landmarks, and far-reaching repercussions of the digital revolution on communication and information sharing in the modern world.

    I. The Past and Present of the Information Technology Revolution

    To early computing devices and the birth of computer networks, we owe the beginnings of the digital revolution in the middle of the twentieth century. The ARPANET, an early version of the internet, the advent of the transistor, and the integration of microprocessors all helped pave the way for the information age we now live in.

    Internet as the Backbone: The internet evolved as a transformative force, linking people around the globe. The World Wide Web, developed by Tim Berners-Lee in 1989, further democratized access to information by allowing people to explore and add to a massive virtual environment. The internet supported the unparalleled communication that fueled the digital revolution.

Developments in Technology, Part II:
The rise of PCs in the '70s and '80s made it possible for homes and small enterprises to have access to powerful computers. Innovations like the graphical user interface (GUI) and the creation of user-friendly operating systems, such as Microsoft Windows and Apple's Mac OS, made computers more accessible and intuitive.

The advent of mobile phones and, later, smartphones completely altered the nature of human interaction with technology. The introduction of the iPhone in 2007 was a watershed moment because it revolutionized the way people communicated, used computers, and passed the time. The widespread availability of apps for smartphones has revolutionized the way in which data is accessed and shared.

Networks for social interaction and information dissemination, such as Facebook, Twitter, and Instagram, have recently come to the fore. Users were able to communicate with one another in real time, sharing text, photographs, and videos with an international audience. The impact of social media on public discourse and interpersonal connections has grown significantly in recent years.

The advent of cloud computing has made it easier and more cost-effective to store and share large amounts of data from anywhere in the world. Services like Amazon Web Services (AWS), Microsoft Azure, and Google Cloud provided scalable and cost-effective alternatives for organizations and people. The transition to cloud storage simplified collaboration and data sharing across multiple environments.

The advent of big data analytics may be traced back to the exponential increase in the amount of digital data produced by a wide range of online pursuits. The processing and analysis of massive datasets became possible with the help of cutting-edge algorithms and machine learning techniques, yielding invaluable insights for businesses, researchers, and decision-makers.

Effects on Interpersonal Interaction:
The advent of digital technology has radically altered human interaction by making communication immediate. With the use of email, IM, and social networking sites, people from all over the world can have instantaneous conversations with one another. The speed of communication has hastened the pace of commerce, diplomacy, and human interactions.

The internet has allowed global connectedness, making cross-border communication and collaboration a breeze. The widespread adoption of video conferencing software like Zoom and Skype has contributed to a newfound sense of global community among professionals and students alike.

Thanks to advancements in digital technology, we now have a variety of communication channels from which to choose to best meet our needs. Individuals can select the most appropriate medium for their communication needs, from text-only emails and phone calls to multimedia-rich apps like WhatsApp and Snapchat.

When it comes to public discourse, social media has leveled the playing field by providing a forum where anybody may voice their opinion to a large audience. However, it has also generated concerns about the dissemination of misinformation, the impact of echo chambers, and the potential for societal polarization.

In spite of digital technology's benefits to communication, it has also presented new difficulties. Misunderstandings are possible due to the instant nature of internet communication and the absence of non-verbal indicators in digital encounters. Also of great worry are the recent developments in areas such as internet privacy, cyberbullying, and digital addiction.

Influence on the Flow of Data:
The proliferation of digital technologies has made formerly restricted information more widely available. Accessing a wealth of information has never been easier than with today's online databases, digital libraries, and search engines. This has had a profound impact on the way individuals learn, conduct research, and find information in their daily lives.

The proliferation of digital mediums has given individuals greater freedom to create and disseminate their own material. Blogs, vlogs, podcasts, and other types of user-generated material have become powerful means for information distribution. This change has prompted citizen journalism and new points of view by posing a challenge to conventional forms of media.

The proliferation of e-commerce platforms enabled by digital technology has fundamentally altered the commercial landscape. Amazon and Alibaba are just two examples of online marketplaces that make it easy for businesses and customers to deal with one another. The convenience of making digital payments has greatly improved internet buying.

By putting a wealth of educational materials on the web, digital technology has revolutionized the educational system. With the advent of e-learning platforms, MOOCs, and virtual classrooms, education has become more accessible to people from all walks of life.

Concerns around data security and privacy have surfaced in light of the rising digitization of information. Digital privacy norms and the necessity for strong cybersecurity measures have been reevaluated in the wake of high-profile data breaches, identity theft, and controversy over the use of personal data by tech companies.

V. Social Consequences:

Despite the increased use of digital technology, a digital divide still exists, resulting in unequal access to the internet and other forms of electronic communication. Inequalities in access are exacerbated by factors such as socioeconomic status, location, and the availability of supporting infrastructure.

Influence on Culture: The Digital Revolution has Changed How We Express Ourselves and What We Buy. The internet has evolved into a medium for artistic and literary expression, facilitating the global distribution of works of art and literature. But people are worried about cultural uniformity and how internet platforms will affect the arts and entertainment industries.

The way people meet and keep in touch with one another has been revolutionized by social networking sites. Although technology makes long-distance communication easier, it has also been linked to negative outcomes like cyberbullying, the need to be always online, and the psychological effects of carefully crafting an online identity.

The dynamics of the workplace have changed as a result of the widespread adoption of digital technologies in the workplace. Workplaces in the digital age depend on remote workers, digital collaboration tools, and virtual communication. The barrier between work and personal life has dissolved, providing both opportunities and challenges for individuals and organizations.

Conclusion:

Every part of modern life has been altered by the advent of new forms of digital communication and information exchange. The digital revolution has brought both unparalleled opportunities and difficulties, from the democratization of information access to the alteration of communication methods. Responsible use of digital technologies requires careful consideration of their societal ramifications, the elimination of access inequities, and the development of guiding ethical frameworks.

The continual evolution of digital technology promises future advances and disruptions. Fostering digital literacy, prioritizing cybersecurity, and encouraging inclusive access will be vital as society continues to adjust to these changes, allowing for everyone to reap the benefits of the digital revolution. In the end, the effect of digital technology on conversation and information exchange reflects the fluid and ever-changing bond between humans and the means they devise to communicate and exchange ideas in the digital age.

- **Exploration of key milestones in the development of computers, the internet, and other technological innovations**

One of the hallmarks of the contemporary era is the rapid development of technology, which has had a profound effect on how people work, live, and interact with one another. This study digs into pivotal points in the evolution of computers, the internet, and other technical developments, charting the development of these tools from their first conceptions to the cutting-edge innovations that define the present.

I. The Earliest Computers and Their Foundations

The earliest known computing device was the abacus, which appeared in ancient cultures around 3000 BCE. Beads or stones mounted on rods were used for simple arithmetic operations. Despite its seeming lack of complexity, the abacus was pivotal in the development of modern mathematics and computation.

Conceptualized by Charles Babbage in 1837, the Analytical Engine is widely regarded as the first mechanical general-purpose computer architecture. Babbage's ideas, notably the use of punch cards for programming, formed the basis for modern computing concepts but were never implemented during his lifetime.

The Telegraph was developed in the 1830s and 1840s. The telegraph's introduction, and especially Samuel Morse's creation of the Morse code, was a huge step forward in the history of communication. The telegraph allowed for the transmission of encrypted messages over electrical wires, paving the way for later developments in the field of long-distance communication.

Invention of the Computer:
General-purpose electronic digital computers can trace their lineage back to the University of Pennsylvania's ENIAC (1946), the Electronic Numerical Integrator and Computer. The ENIAC was a huge computer that was useful in many fields of study and the military.

The UNIVAC I (Universal Automatic Computer) was the first computer to be mass-produced in 1951. UNIVAC I, created by J. Presper Eckert and John Mauchly, was a computer used for both scientific and commercial purposes.

Birth of Transistors (1947): The invention of the transistor by John Bardeen, Walter Brattain, and William Shockley at Bell Labs changed electronics. Smaller, more powerful computers were made possible by the introduction of transistors, which in turn paved the way for the semiconductor industry.

The Third Wave of Computing:
The First Microprocessors Appear in 1971:
The introduction of the Intel 4004 represented a turning point in the history of microprocessors and the beginning of the era of personal computers. Because of microprocessors, computers could be made smaller and cheaper, paving the path for widespread use of the technology.

Apple I's Original Release (1976):
The Apple I, created by Steve Wozniak and Steve Jobs in a garage, is widely considered to be the "birthday" of Apple Inc. It was the first personal computer to come preassembled, marking a paradigm shift toward accessibility and laying the framework for Apple's following breakthroughs.

The release of the IBM Personal Computer (IBM PC) in 1981 ushered in a new era of uniformity in the PC industry. IBM's use of commercially available parts and an open architecture cleared the way for the proliferation of personal computers and the growth of cross-platform software.

The Development of the World Wide Web:
The Advanced Research Projects Agency Network (ARPANET) was established in 1969 as a forerunner to the current internet by the United States Department of Defense. ARPANET pioneered the use of packet switching to facilitate communication between distributed computing nodes.

Information sharing was fundamentally altered with Tim Berners-Lee's creation of the World Wide Web in 1989. The development of HTML, URLs, and HTTP permitted the establishment of a global network of interconnected documents, radically changing how information is accessed and shared.

The 1990s saw the emergence of commercial Internet service providers (ISPs) and the widespread use of browsers like Netscape, marking the beginning of the internet's commercialization. During this time period, the internet expanded from being a restricted network used largely by academics and the military to a worldwide information highway.

Connectivity & Networking Developments:
When Broadband First Began to Be Used:
Broadband internet's widespread usage boosted speeds and connectivity immensely. The availability of high-speed internet has allowed for the smooth distribution of multimedia content, the expansion of online gaming, and the creation of brand-new web-based services.

The growth of mobile networks from 3G to 4G and now 5G has completely reshaped mobile communication. The expansion of mobile applications and services is a direct result of the improvements in mobile network infrastructure, such as faster data transfer rates, lower latency, and more storage space.

The Internet of Things (IoT) is the network of physical objects and digital services that connects our daily lives. This progress has led to the emergence of smart homes, wearable devices, and networked industrial systems, revolutionizing how humans interact with the physical environment.

Advances in 21st-Century Technology:
Significant progress has been made in the fields of artificial intelligence (AI) and machine learning (ML) in the twenty-first century. Industry after industry is being disrupted and

impacted by artificial intelligence (AI) applications ranging from virtual assistants to driverless automobiles.

Secure and transparent transactions have been completely transformed by blockchain technology, which was first introduced in 2008 and is best recognized as the underlying technology for cryptocurrencies like Bitcoin. Beyond banking, blockchain is being researched for applications in supply chain management, healthcare, and digital identity.

Technology advancements in the realms of augmented reality (AR) and virtual reality (VR) have led to more immersive experiences in industries as diverse as gaming, education, and medicine. By simulating surroundings or superimposing digital data over the real world, these technologies present consumers with novel opportunities to engage with digital media.

CRISPR-Cas9, a groundbreaking gene-editing tool, is just one example of the achievements made possible by developments in biotechnology and genetic engineering. These tools have the potential to improve agriculture, cure hereditary illnesses, and solve other urgent problems on a global scale.

Conclusion:
The investigation of major milestones in the evolution of computers, the internet, and technological breakthroughs reveals a constant and accelerated journey distinguished by ingenuity, teamwork, and the relentless quest of progress. Each technological breakthrough, from the advent of the first

computers to the present day of AI and biotechnology, has altered the technical environment and redefined what humans are capable of.

It's important to stop and think about the effects of technological progress on people and the world at large, as well as the ethical questions and duties that come with it. Even more progress will be made in innovation in the future, bringing both exciting opportunities and difficulties that will continue to alter how we live, connect, and imagine the digital age's possibilities.

- **Analysis of the societal changes brought about by the Information Age**

  The rapid progress and broad acceptance of information and communication technologies have ushered in a new era in human history known as the Information Age (also known as the Digital Age). This age, which began in the second part of the twentieth century, has drastically revolutionized the ways in which societies operate, communicate, and interact. The enormous societal changes brought on by the Information Age are explored in this essay, which looks at how these developments have affected areas such as communication, the economy, education, and culture.

  I. The Digital Age of Communication:
  The Information Age has seen a level of global connection never seen before in human history. Due to the proliferation of online communication platforms, the distance between continents has shortened significantly. The advent of modern communication technologies like email, social networking, and video conferencing has made previously impossible relationships routine.

  One of the most defining features of the modern era is the widespread availability of formerly restricted knowledge. The internet has grown into a large library that anyone with access can explore. It has become increasingly difficult for experts in a field to maintain a monopoly on knowledge thanks to the proliferation of online resources like search engines and digital libraries.

The information age has brought about profound changes to the structure and function of traditional media. The rise of online news outlets, blogs, and social media has transformed the landscape of information delivery. The 24/7 news cycle and the increased ability of users to select and organize their own news sources have both hastened the rate at which information travels.

The emergence of social media has transformed interpersonal communication and the dissemination of knowledge. These mediums facilitate communication, information sharing, and creative expression. The spread of false information, invasion of privacy, and the effect on mental health are, nevertheless, emerging as obstacles.

Changes in the Economy, Part II:
The Information Age has seen the digitalization of commerce, which has revolutionized the trade of products and services. Amazon and Alibaba have risen to prominence as e-commerce platforms that provide consumers with the ease of online buying and give businesses access to new international customers.

The emergence of digital technology has contributed to the expansion of the "gig economy," in which more and more people take on short-term, project-based work. Remote work has become increasingly popular as a result of improvements in communication and collaboration technologies. The effects of this change extend to conventional employment models and patterns of urban development.

Big Data and Its Analytical Complements The Information Age ushered in the era of big data. Through the use of sophisticated analytics, the vast quantities of digital data produced every day can be mined for useful information. Companies use big data to refine their methods of decision-making, tailor customer experiences, and advance in the marketplace.

Automation and Artificial Intelligence: Automation and artificial intelligence (AI) have become crucial to numerous sectors. The use of robotics and artificial intelligence in various systems is revolutionizing numerous industries. While these innovations improve productivity, worries about job loss and the ethics of autonomous systems have been raised.

Changes in the Educational Paradigm:
In the Information Age, e-learning and other types of online education have emerged as game-changers in the classroom. Flexibility and ease of access to education are being challenged by the rise of online learning environments such as learning management systems (LMS), massive open online courses (MOOCs), and virtual classrooms.

Personalized Education: Modern tools make it possible to tailor lessons to each student. In order to meet the unique requirements of each student, adaptive learning platforms employ data analytics. This method improves involvement, accommodates various learners' preferences, and makes for a more individualized learning experience.

The advent of the digital age has allowed for a rise in global cooperative educational opportunities. Connecting students and teachers throughout the world allows for the exchange of ideas and experiences. The educational landscape feels more integrated because to virtual collaborations, collaborative initiatives, and online forums.

Dynamism in Culture and Society, Part IV:
A separate digital culture influenced by social media, memes, and online communities has emerged in the Information Age. Trends and consumer behavior are greatly impacted by social media influencers and digital celebrities. However, concerns concerning the effects of artificially constructed online personas on one's sense of identity have been raised.

There are new threats to privacy as a result of the increasing digitalization of society. Concerns about the morality of widespread data gathering and use by tech firms, social networking sites, and other online organizations have prompted discussions on the necessity for strict privacy laws.

The Information Age has given people the tools they need to use the internet to organize and bring about social change. Through the power of social media, movements like #BlackLivesMatter, #MeToo, and climate activism have been able to acquire traction, sparking conversations around the world and galvanizing people to take action.

Inequality in access to digital technologies despite the fact that the Internet has brought together previously isolated populations. The digital divide widens already existing gaps in socioeconomic status, geographic location, and technological opportunity. This gap must be closed if everyone is to have an equal shot at success.

The Effect of Technology on People's Health and Happiness
The widespread implementation of telehealth and digital healthcare solutions during the Information Age has drastically altered the healthcare industry. Accessibility and efficiency in healthcare delivery are improved by tools like remote consultations, health monitoring apps, and electronic health records.

Concerns concerning the effect on mental health have been highlighted in light of the Information Age's ubiquitous connectedness and information overload. In particular, social media has been linked to problems including cyberbullying, anxiety, and the need to constantly adjust one's online persona.

Devices designed to be worn, such as fitness trackers and smartwatches, have proliferated in the modern era of information technology. In real time, users receive information on their physical activity, sleep habits, and other health parameters via these devices.

Conclusion:
The Information Age has ushered in an era of major societal transformations, transforming the way individuals,

communities, and nations work. Technology has had far-reaching effects, as seen by its revolutions in communication, business, and education. Critically examining the societal ramifications, tackling difficulties linked to privacy and inequality, and making sure the benefits of the Information Age are available to all are crucial as we navigate this era of rapid technical innovation.

As technology advances, it will continue to permeate all aspects of society, creating new possibilities and new threats. Societies may successfully adapt to the Information Age and harness the potential of technology to build a more connected, informed, and equal world by encouraging digital literacy, promoting ethical considerations, and maintaining a commitment to inclusivity.

- **Discussion of the challenges and opportunities presented by the digital revolution**

Change on an unprecedented scale has been ushered in by the Digital Revolution, which is defined by the fast development and integration of information and communication technology. The digital revolution has created a new set of difficulties and opportunities, from altering our methods of communication to restructuring entire businesses and social structures. In this article, we'll look at the many facets of this change, from the challenges we confront to the enormous opportunities it presents.

I. The Difficulties Caused by the Digital Age:

A large digital divide has emerged as a result of the information technology revolution, resulting in unequal access to resources and opportunities. This gap exists because of preexisting inequalities and is exacerbated by socioeconomic status, location, and infrastructure constraints. To make sure the benefits of the digital revolution are shared by all, it is crucial to close this gap.

Serious concerns have been voiced about privacy as a result of the widespread adoption of digital technologies. Concerns regarding the morality of data surveillance have arisen due to the widespread collection and use of personal data by tech corporations, social media platforms, and other online entities. Finding a middle ground between progress and protecting people's privacy is essential.

The risk of cyberattacks and data breaches has grown as digital technologies have become more pervasive in every facet of society. Threats to individuals, companies, and governments are posed when bad actors take advantage of holes in the internet's security. Cybersecurity measures and resilience must be continuously improved in response to the ever-evolving nature of cyber attacks.

Job Displacement and Skills Gap: Automation and artificial intelligence have the ability to streamline processes and enhance efficiency but also raise concerns about job displacement. There's a chance that many old occupations could disappear, forcing people to rethink their career goals and acquire brand new sets of skills. Resolving the skills gap and facilitating an orderly labor transition are pressing issues.

The propagation of false information and propaganda has been facilitated by the digital age's decentralized and unchecked transmission of data. In particular, social media sites have become vehicles for the quick spread of disinformation, which can sway public opinion and even elections. Information accuracy and protection from digital manipulation are ongoing problems.

Advantages Made Possible by Technology:
The advent of digital technology has allowed for unprecedented communication amongst people all over the world. In an instant, people from all over the world can communicate and work together thanks to the internet, social media, and other digital communication technologies. Because

of this interdependence, people from different cultures can interact and do business with one another.

Economic Growth and Innovation: Digital technologies are tremendous accelerators for economic growth and innovation. Industry digitization, online retail's meteoric rise, and technological developments like AI all contribute to a flourishing economy. With the use of digital resources, startups and established businesses alike can expand their customer base, boost efficiency, and encourage creativity.

New opportunities for learning and skill development have emerged as a result of the digital revolution, which has had a profound impact on the educational system. Accessible and versatile educational options are made possible by e-learning platforms, online courses, and digital materials. This shift is not only affecting how schools are run, but it is also encouraging students to continue their education throughout their lives and acquire new skills as the world around them evolves.

Technological advances in healthcare have allowed for such novelties as telemedicine, remote patient monitoring, and tailored therapy. These developments improve the quality of care provided to patients, the accuracy of diagnoses, and the availability of healthcare. The integration of health data via digital platforms has the potential to completely alter the nature of medical treatment as we know it.

Inclusive Innovation: The digital revolution has the potential to stimulate inclusive innovation, breaking down barriers and giving opportunity for marginalized communities. Mobile banking, digital literacy initiatives, and online markets give people who were previously marginalized a chance to participate in mainstream economic and social life.

Managing Difficulties While Taking Advantage of Opportunities

Setting up strong regulatory frameworks and efficient governance systems is essential in meeting the challenges of the digital revolution. Governments and international organizations must adjust and create legislation to protect personal data, lessen the likelihood of cyber attacks, and guarantee equitable treatment in the online sphere.

A concentrated effort should be made to invest in digital literacy programs in order to close the digital divide and provide individuals with the skills necessary to thrive in the modern digital environment. To ensure that people of all ages can successfully traverse the digital landscape, it is crucial that educational institutions, governments, and businesses work together.

Concerns about privacy, disinformation, and digital manipulation can only be addressed by placing a premium on ethical design and responsible technology development. The ethical weight, user security, and societal influence of a product or service should be a top priority for any tech company or developer.

Focusing on reskilling and workforce adaptation is crucial as automation and artificial intelligence transform the employment market. Training programs that prepare individuals for new jobs in the digital economy should be jointly provided by governments, businesses, and educational institutions.

Collaboration Across Borders: The Digital Revolution is a Global Phenomenon, Making International Cooperation Necessary. Establishing norms, standards, and agreements that support a secure and equitable digital environment requires collaboration between governments, corporations, and civil society. Cross-border data flows, cyber security, and the oversight of new technology are all areas where cooperation is possible.

The Value of Analyzing Real-World Examples for Improving Performance
Success in Building a Digital Society in Estonia: Estonia is now widely recognized as a global leader in this arena. Digital IDs, online voting, and electronic health records are just a few examples of the ways that e-governance projects in this country have improved access to government services. The success of Estonia is an example of what may be accomplished with a well-planned digital infrastructure and services geared at the general public.

Consequences of the Privacy Breach at Cambridge Analytica:
The Cambridge Analytica incident should serve as a warning against the careless handling of sensitive information. The

unethical mining of Facebook users' information for political profiling exposed the hazards and difficulties of the unchecked use of data online.

Conclusion:
The digital revolution is a complex and ever-changing phenomenon that offers both threats and rewards. Successful navigation of this intricate terrain calls for a preemptive strategy that takes into account the moral, societal, and financial consequences of technological progress. Societies can harness the transformative power of the digital revolution for the benefit of all by utilizing international cooperation, investing in digital literacy, and emphasizing responsible technology development.

It is crucial to encourage a shared dedication to ethical issues, privacy protection, and equitable distribution of benefits as we continue to face the difficulties of the digital age. It is possible for societies to build a future in which the potential presented by the digital revolution are exploited responsibly, leading to a more connected, informed, and equitable world, all via careful governance, technological innovation, and a dedication to digital equity.

Conclusion:

- ## Summarization of the key turning points in human history explored in the book

As we make our way through this book, we are immersed in the rich fabric of human history, a tapestry woven with the strands of discovery, revolt, and significant societal change. Understanding how societies develop, how technologies change lives, and how people adapt to adversity may all be gleaned by studying pivotal moments in human history. In this final section, we'll look back on the major turning points that have molded human history, from the Agricultural Revolution to the Renaissance to the Industrial Revolution to the Age of Discovery to the World Wars to the Information Age.

Leaving behind nomadic hunter-gatherer cultures for more permanent agricultural communities begins with the Agricultural Revolution. The advent of a new era marked by the consistent availability of food brought about by the domestication of animals and the cultivation of plants. This tipping point paved the way for the formation of sophisticated societies, the advent of written language, and the consolidation of existing communities. The farming Revolution paved the way for the rise of civilized societies by shifting human life from nomadic to settled farming practices.

The Renaissance, Part 2: A Renaissance of Art and Learning
Fast forward to the Renaissance, an era of cultural and intellectual renaissance that occurred in Europe over the 14th to 17th century. Interest in classical antiquity was revitalized throughout the Renaissance. The Renaissance was

characterized by a resurgence of interest in humanism, scientific exploration, and artistic expression thanks to the efforts of visionaries such as Leonardo da Vinci, Michelangelo, and Galileo Galilei. The printing press was essential in the spread of ideas, the democratization of information, and the acceleration of the Enlightenment. The cultural environment was reshaped by the Renaissance, and it also set the stage for the scientific and industrial revolutions that followed.

The Industrial Revolution as a Force for Economic and Social Change, III.

The period from the late 18th to the early 19th century, known as the Industrial Revolution, is considered a turning point in human history. Manufacturing, transportation, and social structures were all drastically altered by the transition from rural, manual labor-based economies to industrial, machine-driven output. Steam engines, textile mills, and breakthroughs in iron and steel manufacture spurred extraordinary economic expansion. Challenges, such as labor exploitation, urbanization, and environmental degradation, were also brought into the world during this time period. The advent of modern, industrialized nations, the spread of capitalism, and increased international trade were all made possible by the Industrial Revolution.

Age of Exploration IV: Peering Into the Unknown

From the late 15th to the early 17th century, known as the Age of Discovery, numerous seafaring missions redrawing maps and expanding human knowledge set sail. Perilous travels were undertaken by explorers like Christopher Columbus,

Ferdinand Magellan, and Vasco da Gama, who pushed the frontiers of what was previously known about the planet. These journeys not only paved the way for new commercial routes, but also inspired cultural interactions, scientific breakthroughs, and the mixing of previously separate cultures. The current interconnection of people, goods, and ideas can be traced back to the Age of Discovery.

War's Impact on the Present and Future
Two tragic world wars marred the 20th century and will never be forgotten. The trench fighting of World War I and the resulting shifts in global power helped bring down longstanding empires and pave the way for subsequent political revolutions. The aftermath of the war resulted in the Treaty of Versailles, an attempt to create a new international order that set the stage for more wars. The unparalleled savagery and technological warfare of World War II led to the rise of superpowers, the onset of the Cold War, and the creation of the United Nations to promote international collaboration. These conflicts altered the global power structure and changed the course of many nations and individuals.

The Impact of Technology on Communication and Education
As we enter the 21st century, we find ourselves in the midst of the Digital Revolution, a time marked by the exponential growth of digital technologies. The ways in which we interact socially, learn new knowledge, and do business have all been revolutionized by the advent of the internet, mobile devices, and digital platforms. The knowledge economy has grown and

the world has become more interconnected thanks to this revolution. Concerns about privacy, cybersecurity, and the digital divide are just a few of the difficulties that have arisen as a result. A new chapter in the continuous tale of humankind is being written as the Digital Revolution continues to transform civilizations, economics, and cultures.

Wrapping Up: Consistency and Experience
Certain strands of continuity emerge as we incorporate these major turning events into the vast tapestry of human history. Knowledge seeking, creativity, and a strong will to survive have all survived the test of time. A story of development, adaptation, and interdependence emerges as each turning point builds upon those that came before it.

This investigation into human past yields insights. The Agricultural Revolution teaches us about the transforming power of sustainable food production and settlement. We may learn a lot from the Renaissance's call to embrace the complementary nature of the arts and sciences. As a result of the Industrial Revolution, we now have a responsibility to carefully consider the social and environmental consequences of economic and technological developments. Our global community, rich in diversity and cultural interchange, has much to thank the Age of Discovery for. The World Wars are sobering examples of the devastation that can result from war, and they highlight the need of diplomacy in maintaining international peace. With the advent of the digital age comes the responsibility of using new technologies in a way that protects users' privacy and promotes equal access.

In conclusion, the book's pivotal moments depict the highs and lows, victories and struggles, that have characterized the human experience throughout history. These landmark events help us make sense of the past, understand the present, and plan for the future as a whole. An in-depth knowledge of our history helps us plan for a future that welcomes change, values difference, and meets the difficulties of a globalized society. With so many twists and turns, human history is still being written, and we are all invited to be its authors.

- ### **Reflection on the interconnectedness of these moments and their lasting impact on the world**

  As we consider how a chain of decisive events came together to form the tapestry of human history, the connections between them become clearer. It is impossible to separate the Agricultural Revolution from the Renaissance from the Industrial Revolution from the Age of Discovery from the World Wars from the ongoing Digital Revolution, all of which have impacted the course of human history. In this analysis, we dig into the remarkable interconnection of these moments, investigating how they have not only affected one another but also collectively left an indelible mark on the world, molding communities, economics, cultures, and the very fabric of human existence.

  I. Weaving Together the Past and Present by Following the Threads Between Major Events
  It was the shift from nomadic to sedentary agricultural communities that paved the way for the Renaissance and the subsequent blossoming of cultures and civilizations. The surplus of food made possible the division of labor necessary for the development of higher intellectual activities. As a result of this newfound stability, nations were able to shift their focus from merely surviving to culturally and intellectually flourishing, ushering in the Renaissance. During this time of great change, the arts and sciences flourished thanks to patronage networks that were made possible by an abundance of food.

The Renaissance inspired the Scientific and Industrial Revolutions because of its emphasis on humanism, scientific investigation, and artistic expression. Innovations in equipment and production throughout the Industrial Revolution drew inspiration from the scientific breakthroughs of the Renaissance. The printing press, a product of the Renaissance, was essential in the spread of information, allowing for the quick dissemination of ideas that marked the beginning of the modern industrial period.

Age of Discovery and Industrial Revolution: The industrialization of Europe, spurred by technological advances, necessitated the exploration of other lands in search of raw materials and untapped markets. The Age of Discovery was sparked in part by this need, as well as the desire to find new sources of supply. The economic incentives of the industrialized nations contributed to the growth of maritime exploration. The worldwide trade networks that developed throughout this time period are evidence of the interrelated nature of these epochs, linking previously isolated continents and giving rise to a new era of economic interdependence.

The Age of Discovery and World Wars: The explorations during the Age of Discovery set the foundation for geopolitical developments that played a part in the breakout of World Wars. Tensions and wars emerged as a result of colonial rivalry and imperial ambitions stemming from discoveries and conquests. In turn, the collapse of imperial powers and the emergence of new geopolitical realities following World War I and World War II altered the global political scene.

Devastation wrought by World Wars ushered in a period of global reconstruction and technical progress known as the digital revolution. Competition between the superpowers during the Cold War spurred technological advancement, setting the groundwork for the later Digital Revolution. The geopolitical tensions that defined the World Wars also established the framework for the technological race that ushered in the digital age, therefore the two are inextricably linked.

As a Continuation of the Digital Revolution:
While the Digital Revolution is unmistakable in its own right, it has strong ties to its historical forebears. The technological age expands upon the work done by the scientific and industrial revolutions. Similar to the interconnected trade channels set up during the Age of Discovery, the global nature of digital networks demonstrates this interconnection. The digital age's democratization of information is a continuation of the Renaissance's drive to make information more widely available.

II. Long-Term Effects: How Watershed Moments Reverberate Across Eons
The cultural and intellectual legacy of the Renaissance is inextricably linked to its emphasis on humanism and the pursuit of knowledge. Individualism, creativity, and analytical thought all continue to play significant roles in shaping contemporary culture. The political and artistic climates that

emerged from the period's intellectual ferment set the stage for succeeding upheavals and revolutions.

Changes in the Economy The effects of the Industrial Revolution are still being felt today. Global economic structures have been influenced by the transition from agricultural to industrial and capitalist economies. The entire notion of economic advancement and development is rooted in the transformations brought about by the industrial era, altering trade, production, and consumption patterns.

The Age of Discovery paved the way for globalization by establishing connections between hitherto unrelated regions and their economies. The interconnectedness of modern economies can be traced back to the trading networks developed during this time. Modern international supply chains, financial markets, and cultural interactions can be traced back to the Age of Discovery.

Political Realities and Geopolitical Shifts: The aftermath of the World Wars changed the geopolitical environment. Legacies from this time include the dissolution of colonial empires, the emergence of new nations, and the birth of global institutions like the United Nations. The geopolitical changes paved the way for the ongoing power dynamics that shape international relations.

The technology race sparked by the wars paved the way for the information age we now live in. Technology that defines the modern period was made possible by the collaboration between the military, science, and industry in the middle of the twentieth century. The technological advancements made during the two World Wars have carried over into the modern digital age in many respects.

Turning moments in human history have molded not just political and economic systems, but also the values and cultural mores of the people living in them. Individual rights, equality, and cultural variety are ideas whose origins may be traced back to many ages of human history, and they continue to have an impact on modern communities.

Understanding the Complexity of Our Past to Guide Our Future

Human communities are remarkably flexible and resilient, as evidenced by the interdependence of these watershed moments. The ability to deal with change has been a recurring topic throughout history, from rural areas adjusting to city life during the Agricultural Revolution to post-war reconstruction efforts in developed countries.

Innovation and the pursuit of knowledge have played vital roles in all of these interrelated epochs. The Renaissance encouraged exploration and discovery, laying the groundwork for subsequent advances in science and technology. In turn, the digital age exemplifies the revolutionary impact of knowledge and creativity.

Ethical considerations of progress are prompted by thinking about how different turning points are linked. The lessons of history highlight the significance of combining progress with ethical considerations for a sustainable and fair future, from the environmental consequences of the Industrial Revolution to the ethical considerations of data usage in the Digital Revolution.

Global Cooperation: The interconnection of turning points underscores the need for global cooperation. The risks and rewards of certain eras in history are global in scope. Global cooperation is needed to combat concerns like climate change, cybercrime, and epidemics.

Inclusive Narratives: The examination of interconnected turning moments fosters an inclusive approach to historical narratives. For a full comprehension of human history, it is crucial to acknowledge the contributions and viewpoints of many cultural and community groups. Stories that include all characters strengthen feelings of community and belonging.

Drawing a Cloth from the Threads of Time
These pivotal moments are the colorful threads that have strung together the epic tale of humanity's epic journey. Each epoch, from the beginning of settled agriculture to the present day of digital connection, has expanded upon the achievements of the one before it.

By considering the long-term effects of these landmark events, we become not simply observers of the past but also players in a narrative that is still unfolding. The experiences we've had and the connections we've made have prepared us for a future where flexibility, creativity, and morality will determine our course. The rich tapestry of human history invites us to navigate the present with a keen appreciation for the relationships that unite us across space and time. We all have a part to play in writing the next chapters of this story, and we should do it with an awareness of the interdependence that characterizes our common humanity.

- **Consideration of potential future turning points and their implications for humanity**

  There are defining events in human history that serve to remodel society, redefine standards, and change the course of our collective journey. We are on the cusp of an unpredictable future, therefore it's important to think about potential turning points that could happen and investigate the far-reaching effects they could have on civilization. The future is filled with unknowns, from technology developments and environmental problems to societal transformations and ethical conundrums. However, by looking forward with keen eyes, we can better foresee and manage the contours of what lies ahead.

  Innovations in technology:
  The continuous rate of technological progress is one of the most important forces molding the future. Future decades may see revolutionary advances in fields like AI and biotechnology, which may reshape human existence itself. The development of superintelligent machines, which are superior to humans in every conceivable cognitive task, might mark a watershed moment. The ramifications of such a development are substantial, ranging from tremendous economic disruptions to ethical difficulties regarding the nature of awareness and agency.

  The widespread adoption of biotechnology could also mark a watershed moment. While recent developments in genetic engineering, regenerative medicine, and customized healthcare hold promise for addressing long-standing issues, they also pose ethical questions regarding the appropriate scope of human involvement in nature. Questions about the distribution of these technologies, their accessibility, and their impact on social inequity will become crucial considerations as we traverse this uncharted environment.

Problems with the Environment:
Climate change is an imminent threat that requires global cooperation and immediate action. Environmental disasters, resource scarcity, or a collective realization of the fragility of our world could all contribute to a tipping point in our approach to environmental sustainability. More than only higher sea levels and more intense weather would be affected by this tipping point.

An all-out transition to renewable energy and environmentally friendly activities has the potential to reshape the economy in ways that encourage creativity and new ventures. On the other hand, if environmental problems aren't addressed, it could have disastrous results, such as mass migration from inhospitable areas or resource wars that alter the geopolitical balance of power. How we respond to these environmental concerns will have far-reaching consequences for the future of our species.

Geopolitical tensions, new forms of government, and ideological paradigm shifts are all factors that could trigger a significant turning point in the social and political landscape. Significant changes in the course of human history may be precipitated by a number of events, including the advent of populist movements, the reevaluation of global alliances, and the restructuring of established power structures.

Potential turning points in the sociopolitical domain include the continuous discussion regarding the role of democracy against authoritarianism, the difficulties posed by nationalism, and the search for a more equitable global order. Such changes would have far-reaching effects on people's rights, international relationships, and the fabric of society itself.

Moral Conundrums:
The moral implications of technological and scientific progress are often brought to the forefront by the ethical quandaries that arise as a result of these developments. Concerns about job loss, the independence of intelligent systems, and their possible misuse are all brought up by the progress of sophisticated AI, for example. Ethical guidelines must be built to guide the deployment of AI systems and guarantee they are in line with human values as we near a tipping point when AI could outperform humans.

Challenges surrounding genetic editing, human augmentation, and the very nature of humanity are all at the crossroads of biotechnology and ethics. Our identity and the values we hold as a society will be shaped by the decisions we make as we navigate these ethical problems.

Consequences for the Classroom:
A paradigm shift in how we view education and the sharing of knowledge could have far-reaching effects on our society as a

whole. Personalized, technologically-driven education may be the wave of the future, and the digital revolution has already changed the way knowledge is received.

The increasing popularity of online courses, the use of VR in the classroom, and the priority placed on practical experience rather than formal education are all trends that may signal a sea change in the way that education is practiced. This change has the potential to reshape how people gain access to information, how they acquire skills, and how they are valued in the workplace.

Longevity and Medical Care:
Human lifespan and quality of life may both benefit from medical innovation, particularly in genomics and customized treatment. With advances in anti-aging medicines, organ regeneration, and the avoidance of age-related disorders, it's possible that we've reached a tipping point in the quest for longevity.

Longevity and improved health have far-reaching consequences. Those who choose to work past traditional retirement ages may add to the economy's depth of experience and knowledge. The aging of the population, the distribution of healthcare resources, and the need for new societal structures to support longer lifespans all pose issues.

International solidarity versus protectionism:
Global collaboration vs rising nationalism is a choice that will have far-reaching consequences for international relations.

Pandemics, ecological calamities, or economic failures could be the tipping point that forces people to work together to solve problems. The international system might also be altered if there was a shift toward increasing isolationism and protectionism.

The consequences of these potential scenarios are enormous. In order to effectively solve global concerns, nations must be ready to forego some of their sovereignty and embrace multilateralism. On the other side, nationalism may provide a sense of security and identity but risks increasing global difficulties that require joint solutions.

Conclusion:
It takes a holistic view that incorporates technical, environmental, sociopolitical, ethical, educational, and healthcare facets in order to foresee probable turning points and their ramifications for humanity. We are on the cusp of an unwritten future, and the decisions we make now will have far-reaching consequences.

Our ability to steer towards a future that benefits all of humanity will be measured by how well we are able to strike a balance between the promises of technological innovation and ethical considerations, to address environmental challenges with urgency and foresight, and to navigate social and political shifts with a commitment to justice and equity. The answer comes in our ability to work together, make well-informed decisions, and dedicate ourselves to a future worthy of our highest hopes and ideals.

www.ingramcontent.com/pod-product-compliance
Lightning Source LLC
LaVergne TN
LVHW010218070526
838199LV00062B/4649